Manufactured in the United States of America

ISBN-10   0692350772   ISBN-13   978-0-692- 35077-5

1st Edition, 2nd Printing, May 2015

Printed by Minuteman Press, 335 Main Street, Laurel, MD 20707, USA

eBook available at Kindle Store on Amazon.com and at BN.com as a Nook

    Perfect bound books available at Amazon.com

To order spiral bound books for ease of use in the classroom, the workplace, for research and so Action Literacy Coalitions™ can use i-FLAP™ as an anchor to literally stay on the "same page" when encountering information, email laurel@minutemanpress.com also for multiple copy discounts

- The teaching materials in chapters two and three, can be used right away in the classroom, workplace and for Action Literacy Coalitions as a platform to advance Zurkowski's call for universal IL and AL training. The rubric on page 21, based on 15+ years of testing and refining in the classroom, workplace and daily life, will help teachers grade assignments in all subjects across the curriculum!

- This book is purposely pithy [under 100 pages print edition] in order to avoid contributing to information overload and is written to offer vital information for the IL community, usable materials for teachers and librarians and to empower the general public.

Published by **All Good LiteracieS Press**, publishing arm of the
Global Initiative for Information LiteracieS, Washington, DC, USA
allgoodliteracieS@gmail.com

IL to AL Writings Collection Number 1: 40th Anniversary of IL

Zurkowski's full typewriter typed original report provided by ERIC. Keynotes preserved as submitted by Mr Zurkowski

Mr Jeffrey V Kelly, M.A.T., Teacher, Author and Information Artist at: jeffreyvkelly@gmail.com

Table of Contents   Page

Introduction

Information has existed for a long time and for a long time the inability to consistently gather and act upon good, reliable information has been a problem that has become a major crisis today. The struggle to access, verify and act upon good information is a problem that *Information Literacy* (IL) and *Action Literacy* (AL) help to solve. The power of Information Literacy was unleashed in 1974 when Paul G. Zurkowski, Esq. founded the IL movement at the dawn of the Information Age. As Zurkowski helped form the Information Service Environment he called upon the US National Commission on Libraries and Information Science to establish a program to achieve "universal information literacy" through being literate (learned/functioning) in not only reading and writing but in all facets of information (informed). Consequently, Zurkowski launched a movement that for 40 years has spread throughout the increasingly complex information industry and the world's library science, information science and broader academic communities and is now driving Action Literacy into everyday life around the globe, where more and more people and organizations are empowering their lives using the ideas and skills contained in this book to access, create and take ethical action upon *good* information.

What you have here is *IL to AL Writings Collection Number 1* commemorating the 40th anniversary of the founding of Information Literacy. In this collection you will find: Zurkowski's visionary *Related Paper Number Five* from 1974; a practical IL platform [with the critical thinking code, aaccrr=v@gt&m that is the foundation for Action Literacy and all literacies] for teaching Information Literacy to young students in the classroom, to workers in the workplace and for Action Literacy Coalitions; a practical rubric for teachers and leaders that can be used immediately to evaluate any task or assignment; Zurkowski's four most recent prepared keynote remarks where he lays out his vision for the *next* 40 years where Information Literacy empowers Action Literacy Coalitions to take root in neighborhood libraries throughout the world. Finally, so the original source can be accessed, in the appendix is the "Best Copy Available," preserved by the Educational Resources Information Center (ERIC), United Sates Department of Education, of the original paper Mr Zurkowski himself typed throughout the summer and early autumn of 1974 in Bethesda, MD and at the Information Industry Association (IIA) offices in the shadow of the U.S. Capital, Washington, DC. See what Zurkowski's report looked like, with his hand drawn figures, when it was submitted to the Commission in November of 1974.

Chapter One

The Founding of the Information Literacy Movement, November 1974

"Information is a non-depleting resource and in fact its use enhances its value for users as well as for information...companies [organizations]."

— Paul Zurkowski, *Related Paper Number Five*, ERIC p.17

The Information Service Environment Relationships and Priorities[*]

Paul G. Zurkowski

[*]Originally presented as a report (related paper number five) to the National Commission on Libraries and Information Science for the National Program on Library and Information Services in November of 1974, Washington, DC, USA. Re-published with the permission of Paul G. Zurkowski, Esq. **Converted by Joumana Boustany, Paris Descartes University and edited by Esther Grassian, Fulbright Specialists Program and re-formatted with an introduction by Serap Kurbanoğlu.**

Introduction to Re-Formatted *Related Paper Number 5*

Serap Kurbanoğlu
Hacettepe University, Ankara, Turkey.

When we first decided to organize the ECIL (European Conference on Information Literacy), we started discussing possible keynote speakers for this initial conference. Paul G. Zurkowski, as the creator of the concept of "information literacy," was the first name that came to our minds. However we had neither the courage nor trace of him to contact him personally. I remember writing to Woody Horton, a great supporter from the first day the idea of organizing an international Information Literacy (IL) conference in Europe was born. In my message, I talked about how appropriate it would be if we could bring Mr. Zurkowski to Istanbul to deliver a keynote speech at this very first conference, and how wonderful it would be to hear what he thinks about, and his reaction to developments in the area of IL since he first coined the term in 1974. Good news arrived through Woody, who knew Paul personally and contacted him on our behalf. Paul kindly agreed to travel all the way from Washington, D.C. to Istanbul to address the conference participants. He sent us an abstract for his keynote speech and gave us permission to reprint and disseminate his 1974 Related Paper Number 5.

I have hardly seen an IL resource (book, article, paper, thesis, etc.) which does not cite this report. There is no doubt that his report is one of the most cited works (if not the most cited) in the area of IL. Bibliometric studies which talk about most cited authors and works are not capable of indicating this fact, because they are inevitably based on published works indexed by citation indexes (such as Web of Science and Scopus). Being aware of the value of the report and also its poor condition (a digitally scanned, but faded typewritten paper available through ERIC, with the best available copies hard to read in places), we wanted to create a legible electronic copy that would be easy for non-native English speakers to read, and make it widely available. Once again through Woody, we asked Paul's permission to re-key his report and publish a completely legible copy in the ECIL Book of Abstracts. He was extremely generous to give us permission to do this.

We were excited about the idea of publishing this famous report, however because of its condition; it was not aneasy task to convert it to a Word document. Joumana Boustany from Paris Descartes University converted it to a Word file by using OCR ("optical character recognition") software, with a few words filled in here and there by one of our native English speaking editors, Esther Grassian, Information Literacy Librarian, University of California, Los Angeles, USA.

To help readers follow the text as it appeared in the original report, we put page numbers in square brackets. We did not reproduce the figures since they were produced by hand and therefore have special value. We copied them as they are, indicating the page numbers. We kept the footnotes as they were. All footnotes enumerated by Arabic numerals come from the original text. The rest were created by us/editors. Any additional notes and explanations from the editors appear in square brackets. Typographical errors were also indicated in square brackets.

We hope you enjoy reading it if you have not read it already or re-read it from a clear copy this time.

The Information Service Environment Relationships and Priorities

Paul G. Zurkowski

President, Information Industry Association, Washington D.C., USA, [1969-1989]

National Commission on Libraries and Information Science

National Program on Library and Information Services

Related Paper

Number five

The Information Service Environment Relationships and Priorities

Paul G. Zurkowski

President, Information Industry Association

This paper (1) identifies various categories of private sector information resources; (2) identifies categories of industry/library relations of a traditional nature; (3) identifies examples of situations where traditional roles of libraries and private sector information activities are in transition and (4) suggests priorities for implementation of the National Program to facilitate the recognition and maintenance of the mutually supportive roles of industry and libraries.

November, 1974

The views expressed are those of the author and do not necessarily reflect the position or policy of the NCLIS. Though related to the Commission's National Program, papers in this series are not an integral part of the National Program Document.

Table of Contents

I. Prologue

The Goal: Achieving Information Literacy

Information is not knowledge; it is concepts or ideas which enter a person's field of perception, are evaluated and assimilated reinforcing or changing the individual's concept of reality and/or ability to act. As beauty is in the eye of the beholder, so information is in the mind of the user.

We experience an overabundance of information whenever available information exceeds our capacity to evaluate it. This is a universal condition today for three reasons:

1. The information seeking procedures of individuals are different at different times for different purposes.
2. A multiplicity of access routes and sources have arisen in response to this kaleidoscopic approach people take to fulfilling their information needs. These are poorly understood and vastly underutilized.
3. More and more of the events and artifacts of human existence are being dealt with in information equivalents, requiring retraining of the whole population.

The infrastructure supporting our information service environment transcends traditional libraries, publishers and schools. It embraces the totality of explicit physical means, formal and informal, for communicating concepts and ideas.[1]

From amongst these activities, information publishing activities, whether publicly or privately funded[2] can be identified as those devoted to anticipating information interests, filtering information abundance and directing idea and concepts to specific fields of perception in cost-effective and useful communications media.

Such an information publishing activity can be viewed as a prism. It gathers "light" (ideas and concepts) and performs a variety of "refractory" functions (editing, redacting, printing, microfilming, encoding, arranging, etc.). It produces a spectrum of information products, services and systems designed to correspond to the kaleidoscopic needs of the field of users it purposefully selects to serve. The individual user has many facets and shows different needs to the information sources at different times for different purposes.

Anticipating these changing needs and packaging concepts and ideas to meet them is a major evolving economic activity[***]. (See figure 1). This differs from traditional publishing in significant ways which will be discussed later. (See Figure 2).

Figure 1 demonstrates that information publishing activities *gather data* of interest to a specific subject, field or market, *produce information* [sentence ends here, without a dot].

---

[1] Including but not limited to telephone, television, radio, human voice, and action, newspapers, magazines, books, paperbacks, movies, theater, graffiti, pamphlets, maps, tours, audio tapes, schools, door-to-door salesmen, direct mail advertising, computer data bases, newsletters, microform collections, drugstore book and magazine racks, government pamphlets, bookstores, libraries, political campaigns, churches, social clubs, satellite communications, cable television, other broad band communications, cocktail parties, town criers, committees of correspondence, pamphleteers, museums, expositions, etc. *Most importantly, however, the infrastructure also includes all of the human skills necessary to the functioning of these physical means, as well as the wide variety of economic structure on which their continued viability depends.*

[2] The Information Industry Association (I.I.A.) was established in 1968 and is made up today of more than 70 member companies. The I.I.A. is limited by its charter to commercially chartered, for-profit companies, but the functions of the industry are also performed by non-profit and government agencies. See also *Encyclopedia of Library and Information Science*, Vol. II Marcel Dekker, Inc., New York, 1974, p. 483 et seq.

[***] Editor's note: Many parts of the original report are underlined. Here all underlined parts are presented in italics.

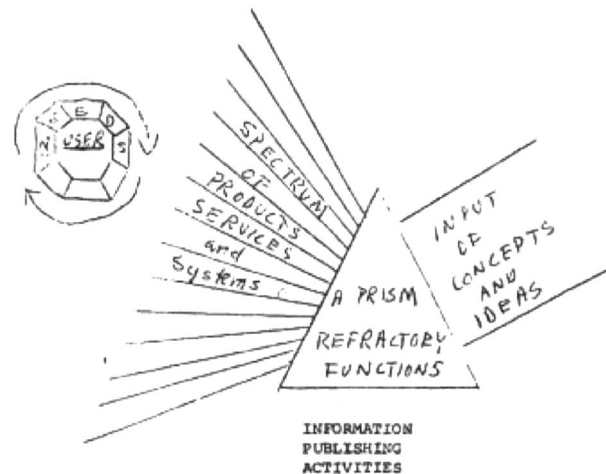

Figure 1 [page 3]

These include:

A. *Information Generation:* 1. Original authoring or writing (e.g., NY Times); 2. Compilation (e.g., Dunn and Bradstreet, R.R. Bowker; 3. Recruitment of authors (e.g. Alfred Knopf); and 4. Cataloging, abstracting, and indexing (e.g., any "secondary service" publisher, like Congressional Information Service or H. W. Wilson).

B. *Information Publishing:* 1. Editing (all of the above); 2. Formatting for original publication (all of the above); 3. Formatting for re-publication in another form (e.g., CIS Microfiche Library; The Readers Guide Bantam Books; Lockheed on-line system); 4. Distribution (e.g., Richard Abel; Lockheed; McNaughton Library Service); and 5. Publicizing, marketing, and educating (all of the above).

C. *Technology Applications:* ("Hardware"): can be applied in the pursuit of any of the above functions; these include such things as dictating machine, microfilm camera or reader, computer composition microwave transmission, printing press, computer storage and retrieval[,] optical character recognition, etc.

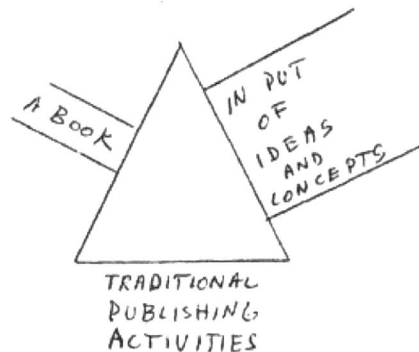

Figure 2 [page 4]

A traditional publisher considers each book an economic entity standing alone. The publisher is successful to the extent that more books succeed than fail. In traditional publishing, the related, parallel portions of the spectrum of products and services which can be derived from the input of ideas and concepts may or may not be recognized and may or may not be marketed.

[page 5]

[Line missing] (products, services or systems capable of informing) *and focus the information* on the intended users expected needs. All of these are labor intensive, intellectually disciplined, costly, risky and capital intensive activities. Their success is measured by the feed-back received from the user.

In a vital marketplace of ideas information publishing activities must enjoy not only the right to succeed but also the right to fail.

In the competitive information marketplace the measure of success is whether a particular enterprise proves to be profitable. The marriage of the profit motive to the distribution information is the single most important development in the information field since Carnegie began endowing libraries with funds to make information in books and journals more widely available to the public.

Since no one can have a monopoly on ideas and concepts (copyright grants only a limited monopoly in a particular statement of ideas or concepts), *competition is keen* in identifying ideas and concepts with a high degree of relevance to a particular market or group of users and in bringing those ideas and concepts into the field of perception of that market. If the right decisions are made about (a) the identification of ideas and concepts (b) their documentation or packaging, (c) the intended group of users and (d) pricing, the enterprise will thrive and be profitable. *If not it will fail.*

"Precisely because business can make a profit; it *must* run the risk of loss. The strongest argument for "private enterprise" is not the function of profit. The strongest argument is the function of loss. Because of it business is the most adaptable and the most flexible of institutions around. It is the one that has a clear, even though limited, performance test. It is the one that has a yardstick".[3]

[page 6]

In the government sector no such yardstick exists. Information activities are funded as a value of society. This is a more general standard and one more subject to the laws of inertia.

"One can argue that this or that obsolete hospital is really needed in the community or that it will one day again be needed. One can argue that even the poorest university is better than none. The alumni or the community always has a "moral duty" to save 'dear old Siwash'.

"The consumer, however, is unsentimental. It leaves him singularly unmoved to be told that he has a duty to buy the product of a company because it has been around a long time. The consumer always asks: 'And what will the product do for me tomorrow?' If the answer is 'Nothing' he will see its manufacturer disappear without the slightest regret."[4] Thus, for the user, there is a specified yardstick. *Information has value in direct proportion to the control it provides him over what he is and what he can become.*

The user is willing to pay for services which enhance his control. Not everyone perceives this as a measure of the value of information. Many who are conscious of the need for information still feel that information, like air, is a free good.

People trained in the application of information resources to their work can be called information literates. They have learned techniques and skills for utilizing the wide range of information tools as well as primary sources in molding information solutions to their problems.

The individuals in the remaining portion of the population, while literate in the sense that they can read and write, do not have a measure for the value of information, do not have an ability to mold information to their needs, and realistically must be considered to be information illiterates.

Figure 3 illustrates the relatively small percentage of people who have attained some degree of information literacy.

---

[3] *Age of Discontinuity* - Peter F. Drucker; Harper & Row, 1969, p. 237 et seq.

[4] *The Age of Discontinuity*, op. cit.

PERCEIVED
VALUE OF INFORMATION

MEDICAL, GOVERNMENTAL
BUSINESS, SCI/TECH
INFORMATION LITERATES

U. S. POPULATION

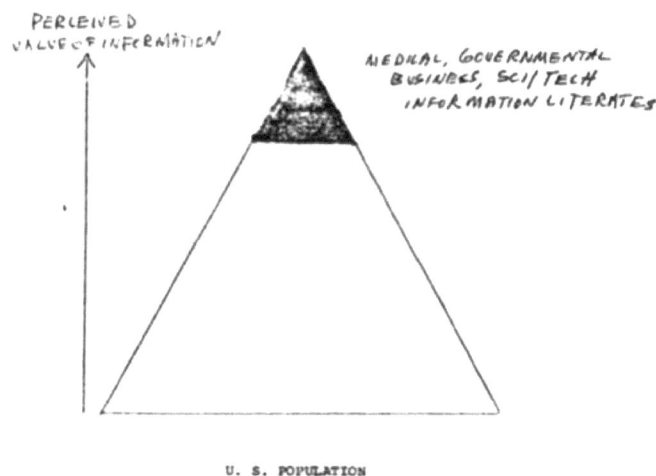

Figure 3 [page 7]

While the population of the U.S. today is nearly 100% literate, only a small portion - perhaps one-sixth, could be characterized as information literates.

[page 8]

The work of the Commission should be viewed in terms of achieving total information literacy for the nation.

This paper seeks to:

1. Provide indicators of the broad range of services already being offered by non-government, non-library-based business firms.
2. Identify the policy questions that need to be resolved in order to maximize the pluralistic structure of the information economy already in place in order to achieve information literacy for our entire population, and
3. Suggest priorities which the commission should consider in attaining the goal of information literacy.

II. *Private Sector Information Resources*

A snapshot of the private sector information resources needs to be taken with an extremely wide angle lens. Having taken the picture it is fairly easy to identify and define categories of services, subject areas covered, and, in-some cases, even the intended markets for particular products. Specific categories will be identified and examples cited for each without any expectation that the list will be complete.

It must be noted, however, that each resource cited is but one of a group in a spectrum of services offered by a particular company and its competitors and that for each resource cited there exists, in various stages of development, another spectrum of comparable, related or competitive services (cf. Figure 1.).

A. *Information Banks*

The creation of an *information bank* – a resource people can draw on, is a *most* capital intensive activity.

The Library of Congress MARC program is one example.

[page 9] Others include:

Shepard's Citations - used in law libraries and by individual law firms, based on the arrangement of legal citations to previously decided court cases.

Science Citation Index and *Social Science Index*[5] used in research libraries and by individuals, based on an organization of scientific citations in sci/tech literature and social science literature, respectively.

International Data Corporation - monitors the location of computer facilities in the U.S. and elsewhere identifying central processing units and related facts about each facility. Its market is primarily suppliers of computer room equipment services and supplies.

Predicasts, Inc. - a Cleveland based company, monitors the literature of the business world and captures one-line entries on specific articles industries by SIC code numbers to facilitate users seeking information on specific industrial and business fields.

Disclosure, Inc. of Silver Spring, MD., has created a machine readable file of abstracts covering all the corporate reports required to be filed with the Securities and Exchange Commission. The information files are published regularly in ink print as a form of bibliographic control over the microfilm version of the documents also marketed by Disclosure. The arrangement was achieved through solicitation of competitive sources by SEC that resulted in a no-cost to the government contract. The latest contract renewal included a provision for pilot programs in Dallas and **[page 10]** Nashville where library use of the financial information provided by Disclosure developed new customers for the libraries. Subsequently, these two libraries have subscribed to the Disclosure Service to continue serving their users.

Standard and Poor's - a McGraw-Hill Company, has collected a great deal of detailed income statement and balance sheet data on public companies, data which were not compiled and easily available anywhere else to the public.

The New York Times Information Bank - includes full texts of the informative abstracts written on all articles appearing in the *New York Times.*

The government subsidized the creation of a wide-range of sci/tech data bases by professional societies. These include Engineering Index, Chemical Abstracts, American Physics Institute and others.

Many of these information banks are marketed respectively by each company in a variety of formats and initially were offered only in ink print.

There are a dozen companies which have built information banks, in part based on the MARC tapes, offering a multitude of services to libraries. Information Dynamics Corp., Richard Abel & Co., Science Pres., Inc., Brodait, are but a few.

B.   *Information Bank Vendors*

The last 18 months has seen the emergence of companies marketing access to machine readable information banks. The function of these companies is to make arrangement to have available for on-line search as many **[page 11]** information banks as possible. They then seek to develop a dual multiplier effect in marketing access to these banks. The more banks a company has "up" the easier it is to convince a user to install the necessary terminal equipment by which to gain access to the files. Similarly, the more there is to search the more likely it is the searches will be made.

Lockheed Information Systems, Systems Development Corporation and certain time-sharing organizations such as General Electric vend access to multiple information banks stored in their systems based on a variety of lease and user charges.

Lockheed is experimenting with several Northern California libraries under a National Science Foundation grant to determine the feasibility of having libraries serve as "retail" outlets for these search services. Presumably, the cost of these search services would ultimately have to be borne either by the library or its users.

A further innovation both Lockheed and SDC offer their subscribers who perform searches on information files created by the Institute for Scientific Information is the facility to order a tear sheet of any article they obtain a citation on from the system. The orders are stored in the vendor's computer and are "read out" by ISI at the end of the day. Original Article Tear Sheets or authorized photocopies are supplied by ISI by return mail. This arrangement provides one example of how to deal with the threshold copyright problem, since ISI has established relationships on copyright questions with, and pay royalties [sic] to, the publishers of journals cited in its information bank file.

The New York Times Information Bank is unique in that the creator of the Bank is also vending access to it by placing terminals and training **[page 12]** people in their use. The *Times* is experimenting in Canada with providing individuals access to the files through libraries.

The availability of such services in libraries has numerous side effects:

---

[5] Both are products of the Institute for Scientific Information, Phila.

1. For information bank creators and vendors who originally designed their service and priced it on a "per-search" basis increased usage in libraries widens the market.
2. For creators and vendors whose costs have never been subsidized and also serve a narrow market, the ability of users to gain access to the file on a "per-use" basis without paying lease fees charged other users destroys the economic basis of the file and will eventually eliminate its availability or result in severe modification in the file and its marketing procedures.
3. In some cases where access to the machine readable version requires the use of an ink-print version, library usage will expand markets for both.
4. In cases where the availability of the machine readable file on a per-use basis is an adequate substitute for the ink-print versions, there is serious cause for concern on the part of the publisher who has an economic activity in ink-print but may lose out if the machine readable file becomes available even on a "per-use" basis in libraries.

C.   Publishers

Libraries are filled with the products of publishers, books, journals, pamphlets, recordings, film strips, microfilm collections. All are economic goods which have been purchased by libraries for the express purpose of lending them to the patrons of the libraries. When these items are out on loan they are off the shelf. If demand increased in the past additional copies were purchased.

In many cases this lending practice created an awareness of the value of the information contained in the materials and often led to individuals **[page 13]** subscribing directly on a personal basis for similar services. In the case of many business information services this led to the development of a whole market for timely services.

Many publishers offer discounts to libraries considering the library a ready market and one requiring lesser marketing expense to reach. Other publishers, primarily of reference and information tools scale their subscription rate to the anticipated number of users expected to have access to their products. In any case, the pricing strategy is designed to generate sufficient revenues from a multitude of sources to make it economic to undertake the creation, manufacture and distribution of a particular product.

A starting point for this strategy is the identification of "first copy costs", or what does it cost to create the first copy? (After one copy is made, the incremental costs of subsequent copies are usually comparatively small.) The economics of publishing requires that all subscribers pay a share of these first copy costs. Since the first copy costs are to be incurred, regardless of the medium used for publication, many journal publishers contend that spreading these over the largest ink-print press run possible is the most cost-effective means of distributing scientific and technical information.

In the field of publishing there also is a relatively new phenomenon called micropublishing, or more correctly microrepublishing, since it almost universally involves republishing ink-print materials, both under copyright and in the public domain in microform.

Information Handling Services organizes, indexes, and microfilms on **[page 14]** 16 mm cartridge film engineering and construction catalog information. Its contribution is to organize and make readily accessible a large body of otherwise wise elusive and quickly dated materials.

Congressional Information Service abstracts, indexes and microfilms nearly one-half the total output of the Government Printing Office. Two basic corpora of documents includes all Congressionally generated reports, hearings, bills, etc. (except The Congressional Record which is microrepublished by University Microfilms, Princeton Microfilms and others) and statistical publications of all government agencies. CIS recently began offering a file containing copies of all bills offered in Congress at a price substantially below the product of the Library of Congress it replaced. Its breakeven point is approximately 15 subscribers. (In the information service environment small audiences can be served economically and competitively.)

Readex Microprint republishes the complete output of the Government Printing Office in a micro-opaque medium for which it also offers a reader/printer.

Research Publications, Inc. collects and microfilms large academic collections such as the Papers of The Confederacy and the League of Nations Documents. It also offers a microfilm on all patents issued by The Patent Office and has begun filming state documents. It provides detailed indexes with which to use its products.

University *Microfilms*, has collected U.S. doctoral theses on microfilm and has created a Dissertations Abstracts publication by which to identify relevant theses. It also markets to libraries authorized microfilm versions of most popular periodicals.

Bell and Howell Microphoto microfilms large numbers of newspapers including a whole co-action on the underground press.

Greenwood Press micropublishes large collections of a retrospective nature and also offers a service on municipal documents.

Disclosure, Inc., U.S. Historical Documents Institute, Microfilming Corporation of America and Library Resources, also offer a variety of micro-published materials.

This is a relatively new industry dating back only to the years immediately prior to World War 2. It is an industry that has learned that to stay in business it must do more than create on film that which already exists in ink-print; it must add value by what it does. This value most often takes the form of one or all of the following:

1. Collecting as complete a set as humanly possible from many disparate sources.
2. Organizing, editing and arranging the material.
3. Filming and coding the material on film.
4. Creating tools by which users can locate on the microfilm the precise information they desire promptly and easily.

In many cases the first copy costs of these collections must be spread over a maximum expected sale of 15 to 20 copies.

D.   Information By-Products

These include everything from SDI services to journals, newsletters and other serial products. They might be by-products of an information bank or a micropublishing or publishing venture.

One major business --- Dodge Information Systems --- a McGraw-Hill Company, fits in this category. The Dodge people serve the construction field. They **[page 16]** have a data base consisting of all construction jobs being undertaken in the U.S. of a certain minimum size. The file contains information such as date bids are due, who was awarded the contract, when various subcontracts will be let, who the subcontracter is and when he is expected to buy light bulbs, etc.

Information is sold out of this file to all kinds of users who wish to compete for the business of supplying materials to builders. This is sold in little pieces of paper on a daily basis, on user pre-printed multiple copy computer forms for use by salesmen and their managers in keeping track of business in a territory, etc.

Obviously, this information gives a salesman great control over who he is and what he can become. It has great value.

Newsletters are another "by-product," but more a by-product of the data base building process than of the completed data base. A newsletter has value because it becomes built into the user's life style. It repeatedly gives him ideas and concepts that are relevant. The newsletter publisher maintains good "feedback" from his users and knows whether what he puts out is used, and, if not, why not, and how to correct it. That is data base building. People who have been doing this for a long time have a natural reserve of information that should be convertible to a database.

This, in turn, can then be repackaged as books, as SDI, as on-line retrieval information, as complementary data bases to other files also "up" on the same system, etc. While there are data conversion costs involved, the most expensive functions – data acquisition and editing--have been done and paid for. In addition the information has been validated through demonstration and repeated use.

Information is a non-depleting resource and, in fact, its use enhances its value for users as well as for information publishing companies.

E.   Information Evaluation

It, too, embraces a multitude of activities. It includes, for example, facilities management, such as the *Informatics* operation of the NASA Space Information Center, where the world of space-related information is evaluated, managed and distributed. *Herner & Co.* runs a similar facility for Walter Reed Army Medical Center, concentrating on managing bio-medical research results for the U.S. Army. *Aspen Systems* has operated more limited facilities for specific task-oriented activities creating an information capability in support of certain inquiries by regulatory agencies of government.

Another example of the information evaluation activities of the industry is the whole phenomenon of "user generated", or custom query "on demand" information companies. A prime example is FIND, operated   by

Information Clearing House, N Y. There are probably 20-30 companies of this kind in the U.S. today operating on a commercial basis. There are at least as many operated by government and non-profit ventures as well.

The economic reality giving rise to this business is the multi-disciplinary approach all businesses are forced to take today. Libraries in business locations turn out to have finite personnel and holdings. Rather than augment both and build into their cost structure permanent high levels of activities, many businesses are choosing to rely on the "expert access" [page 18] to information these firms provide. (They serve a similar function to that of the temporary help firms).

In addition, if one of these on-demand companies has 500 industrial subscribers it probably recognizes that to be a valid statistical sample of the U.S. market for information. If a dozen companies out of those 500 ask about the same question in one week, this triggers certain developments: (1) The question is researched 12 different ways. (2) The researchers identify the fact that this subject probably is of interest to a large number of other companies, both subscribers and non-subscribers. (3) A special report is prepared as a by-product of the earlier research and is sold. (4) The research itself, without regard to the source of the questions, may be used to construct a data base for other users as well.

Also in this information evaluation field is the whole area of special reports such as those created by Frost & Sullivan, Predicasts, Quantum Science, International Data Corporation, Auerbach, Business International, etc. In the sense that specialized (mostly sci/tech) journals also carry evaluated (by peers) information, they too fall in this category.

III.   Traditional Library/Industry Relationships

In the age of evolving reading literacy library/industry relations were mutually beneficial.

Libraries were and still are for many companies the principal market for published products. For many products, the existence of a fairly certain library market for a book or journal assured a la large press run distributing first copy costs widely and reducing retail prices for individuals [page 19] as a result.

Libraries with collections of materials and subscriptions to current periodicals also form a market for publishers of reference works and for current awareness services. Both such products rely on the ready availability within the library of a fulfillment capability to complete the current awareness/fulfillment cycle essential to the complete information process.

For newer, innovative products libraries offer the traditional service of training individual users in the use of new products.

IV.   Transitional Library/Industry Relationships

What is characterized in the Report as the threshold question - copyright - covers a wide range of ways in which the library/industry roles are in transition.

For the journal publisher, interlibrary loans via photocopies represents a reversal of the relationship by which sufficiently large press runs resulted in distributing first copy costs broadly over all or almost all users. Current practice resulting in reduced multiple subscriptions within each library have drastically reduced the number of subscriptions from which first copy costs can be recovered.

The further practice of photocopying portions of journals, thereby eliminating the need for users or satellite or borrowing libraries to subscribe has the following result. (See Figure 4).

[page 20]

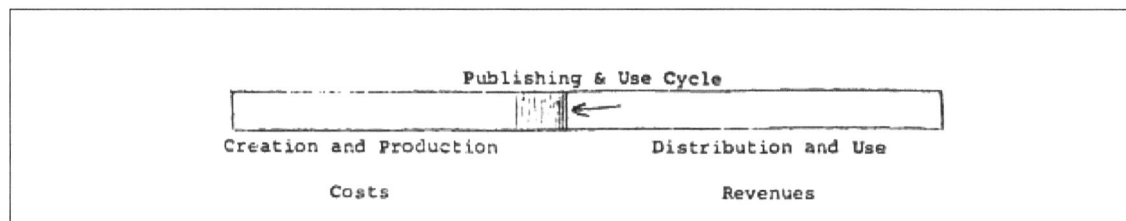

Publishing & Use Cycle

Creation and Production   Distribution and Use

Costs   Revenues

[Figure 4 - page 20]

In the publishing and use cycle the major costs are associated with creation and production. Revenues are generated from the distribution and end use. Photocopying, while not generating revenues for libraries, does push the publisher farther and farther back into the cost area and out of distribution and revenue area.

In many situations libraries by marketing their services to commercial users in industrialized locations on a subsidized basis are competing unfairly with firms which must recover capital investment, pay a return on investment (prime rates remain high for venture capital), and pay state and federal taxes. The change represented by this example is one of scale of activity rather than in kind. Often in order to "get a good return for the taxpayers investment in a new information service" libraries will seek to reach out to precisely the same people to whom the private sector is seeking to market similar or even identical services.

Superficially both are serving the same objective - raising the information literacy of the U.S. population. From an economic standpoint, however, there is a real danger that this kind of unfair competition will destroy the economic viability of the creator of the service involved and his business will fail. Government funding will became the only viable way of creating such information services. By comparison, consider what the **[page 21]** impact on freedom of expression would have been as the U.S. developed reading literacy if government funding had been the only viable way of publishing books and journals.

A major feature of transitional library/industry relations, thus, is that both libraries and information companies are seeking to serve the same users of very specialized services.

This would be further aggravated by the creation of a national system for sharing resources unless ways were clearly defined for achieving optimum utilization of both resources.

Other than photocopying is involved in this area. For a micropublisher of a large academic collection of materials, the sharing among major research libraries of key portions of the microfilmed collections can be fatal to the economic viability of the collection if as much as one of the 15-20 potential sales are lost. A national system of sharing would guarantee that result in every case. Here again specific ways must be found to assure continued viability of multiple sources of materials.

In the case of federal libraries their redesignation as information centers also represents a real threat not only to industry but to the national tax base as well. Many federal information centers offer subsidized information services to an ever widening circle of users - first, other government agencies, then, state agencies, then, government contractors, then, their subcontractors and then on ad infinitum.

Not only does this preempt large markets for direct sales to these same users of information services, but it creates a larger federal bureaucracy and denies tax revenues to both state and federal treasuries.

It is significant that the first congressional policy statement on **[page 22]** government competition with the private sector should have come in 1933. In the depth of a depression, when Congress was cutting its salaries, it is logical that the Congress would recognize the hazards to the tax base of government agency preemption of private sector opportunities.

The size of the impact on tax revenues was set forth in a Department of Commerce table at 60 of the Report of the Commission on Government Procurement. The Commerce Department estimated that in 1970 there were $4 billion of services performed by the government that could have been shifted to the private sector.

The report states this would have produced an additional $25 to $35 million in tax revenues to the states alone. In fiscal 1970 the government agencies reported $7 billion of similar services that were performed in house rather than contracted out. If $5 billion of that had been shifted to the private sector the taxes paid to the U.S. Treasury would have totaled up to $250 million.

V.   Policy Questions

In the "Reading Service Environment" the basic policy issue: what portion of publishing and library services should be left to be satisfied by operation of the forces of the marketplace and what portion must be subsidized was fairly clearly defined. In fact, the subsidized portion operating by resource sharing aggregated dependable, continuously-funded markets for publishers who, thus, became secondary beneficiaries of the subsidy. Economies of size were assured and a stable, well-balanced system evolved to serve the reading public.

This complex of relationships constituting the Reading Service Environment **[page 23]** in the main provided a healthy, dynamic institutional framework for harnessing the nation's pluralistic resources to the task of creating a reading literate society and a competitive marketplace of ideas. In many respects this relationship still pertains and it is in the public interest for all concerned to continue to build on this mutuality of interest in extending information literacy to the all segments of society.

With the introduction of new information processing technologies the line between marketplace and subsidized functions in some respects has become blurred. The process of achieving information literacy involves defining that line clearly and realistically, and in defining an institutional framework for the Information Service Environment. In our age of information overabundance, being information literate means being able to find what is known or knowable on any subject. The tools and techniques and the organizations providing them for doing that form this institutional framework. Three major time tested policies contributed to the success of the Reading Service Environment and their application to the Information Service Environment is essential to its successful operation:

1. Individual fulfillment, the advancement of knowledge and the discovering of truth, participation in decision making by all members of society, and achieving an adaptable and stable community depends on a system of freedom of expression.[6]

2. Government should not perform services for citizens which citizens are capable of performing for themselves.

3. Government has a legitimate responsibility for assuring educational opportunities for all.

[page 24]

A.   The System of Freedom of Expression Basis for the Information Service Environment

"Congress shall make no law...abridging the freedom of speech or of the press..." First Amendment, U.S. Constitution.

"A system of freedom of expression *** is a group of rights assured to individual members of 'the society to form and hold beliefs and opinions on any subject, and to communicate ideas, opinions and information through any medium * * * from the obverse side it includes the right to hear the views of ethers and to listen to their version of the facts * * * the full benefits of the system can be realized only when the individual knows the extent of his rights and has some assurance of protection in exercising them * * * it does not come naturally to the ordinary citizen, but needs to be learned. It must be restated and reiterated not only for each generation but for each new situation. It leans heavily upon understanding and education, both for the individual and the community as a whole.

"Thus it is clear that the problem of maintaining a system of freedom of expression is one of the most complex any society has to face, self-restraint, self-discipline, and maturity are required. * * * The members of society must be willing to sacrifice individual and short-term advantage for social and long-range goals.

Second (among legal doctrines supporting a system of freedom of expression) is the utilization and simultaneous restriction of government in regulating conflicts between individuals or groups within the system of free expression; in protecting individuals or groups from non-government interference in the exercise of their right to expression; and in eliminating obstacles to, or affirmatively promoting effective functioning of the system. * * * Development of this concept involves formulating specific rules for mutual accommodation of participants in the system, fairness in allocation of scarce facilities and assurance that the system will be expanded rather than contracted."[7]

The practical policy implications for achieving information literacy of a system of freedom of expression are:

1. Resource sharing in the Information Service Environment differs by an order of magnitude and has the opposite impact on sources **[page 25]** of materials to that which it had in the Reading Service Environment. Instead of aggregating markets for suppliers of materials it disaggregates these markets and denies compensation to suppliers for their services. This destroys the economic foundations of the suppliers and reduces pluralism in choices available to citizens. Systematic photocopying of published materials amounts to republishing and requires copyright clearances. All parties should work together to resolve this threshold question.

2. In-house or captive development of systems capability denies the entire (not just the library) community the benefit of competition among suppliers. (Services developed outside the library community can be sold to non-library users and the cost be amortized more broadly.) Services for inter-library cooperation should not be contracted for on a sole source basis. Competitive procurement should be required to obtain competitive bids on the specifically described services desired.

3. A concomitant of freedom of expression is the need for the user to have confidence in the information source on which he proposes to rely. Subsidization of activities that preempt alternative sources eliminates one base for confidence: Competition among products delivering concepts and ideas.

4. Individuals require not only the right to speak, but also to be heard. A pluralism of channels for communication must therefore be preserved. This will require restraint on the part of subsidized activities so as not to preempt opportunity or to eliminate channels for communication alternative to subsidized channels.

5. There must be a clear policy statement favoring alternative **[page 26]** channels for communication since in its absence the risk capital needed to sustain alternate channels will not be forthcoming. For pluralism to be assured there must be assurance that the system will be expanded rather than contracted.

---

[6] Thomas I. Emerson, *The System of Freedom of Expression*, Random House, 1970, p.3 et seq.

[7] Thomas I. Emerson. *The System of Freedom Expression* op. cit

B. Government Services

Government should not perform services for its citizens which the citizens are capable of performing themselves. The benefits of this policy are:

1. That private, competitive services arise to offer citizens a choice of services.
2. That the private services offered amortize first copy costs against all possible users rather than only those government would serve with its products.
3. That the tax base is broadened by policies encouraging private initiatives and the investment of private risk capital in the development of capital intensive activities.
4. That it is more cost-effective for government to rely on private risk capital investments. If one agency requires a service needing $2 million in capital investment, by relying on private risk capital it can reduce its costs to a pro rata share of that cost distributed among all users.

The Government of the U.S. also has the responsibility to assure that the opportunity for private sector initiatives is expanded and not contracted. This should be implemented through policies affecting the procurement policies and competitive activities of the instrumentalities the government chooses to fund to implement its objectives.

Since there currently is no national agency charged with the responsibility for overseeing the formulation, implementation and oversight of government policies in this area, it is all the more important that the **[page 27]** Commission enunciate a policy identifying goals for government activities in the information service field which will direct the energies of people in government in supportive rather than competitive activities.

C. Education

Much of what has been stated above pertains to the estimated one-sixth of the U.S. Population that is information literate. The priorities of the Commission should be directed toward facilitating the participation of the pluralistic segments of the Information Service Environment already serving that segment of society. Capital investment by government in developing further resources to serve that share of the population would necessarily come at the expense of the five-sixths of the population that lacks the training to be literate in an information sense.

The top priority of the Commission should be directed toward establishing a major national program to achieve universal information literacy by 1984.

This would involve the coordination and funding of a massive effort to train all citizens in the use of the information tools now available as well as those in the development and testing states. The pattern of growth in this field is well established and should be built upon to expand the overall capability of all U.S. Citizens. Such an effort would necessarily create many new opportunities, some of which would be appropriate to the marketplace and others for subsidy.

Until the population as a whole is prepared to utilize and benefit across the board from the capabilities of the Information Service Environment proposals to create systems, serving the elite alone will lack the popular political support needed to obtain the level of government funding suggested in this Report to the Commission.

Chapter Two

From Theory to Action!

The following IL foundational teaching materials through page 21, were created to be used as a platform and reference point when encountering information in the classroom, the workplace, daily living and for Action Literacy Coalitions to further Zurkowski's historic aim of spreading Information Literacy...and now also Action Literacy!

"Well, what good is being information literate if the information or wisdom is not used for good?"

— Paul Zurkowski, from his interview on his trip to Turkey and the First ECIL, October 2013

"The research...shows that as people go about learning they interact with information in different ways. They may be learning about a content area in a formal context, they may be engaged in informal learning as they go about their daily life, or they may be learning through doing original research."

— Dr. Christine Bruce, *Informed Learning*. Association of College and Research Libraries/American Library Association, Chicago, 2008.

in-Formation Literacy Action Platform™ by Jeffrey V. Kelly, M.A.T.

Information Literacy is: *"The ability to extract, accept, and create good value from needed information."*

Critical Thinking Code™ by JVK **a a c c r r = v @ g t & m**

±**a** ccurate/authentic,

Notes: _____

±**a** ccessible, appropriate, anti,

_____

c ontext, concepts, compare & contrast,

_____

±**c** lear, complete, customize, confirm, choice,

_____

±**r** elevant, repeatable, reliable,

_____

±**r** efined, reference point,

_____

= (equals)   SUBJECT ➜ _____ ⬅ FOCUS

PROBLEM/DECISION/TOPIC/ISSUE

v alue, validate, verify, veracity,

@ (at)

g ood/goal,

t ime/timely, truth,

& (and) **m** iscellaneous, helpful/harmful, ethical, opposite, emotions, perspective, balance, love, currency, data, conscious,

The Vote/Continuum

- Input ➜ Processing ➜ Output
- **70-10-10-10** perspective
- Change *IS* UnChanging
- Awake *OR* Asleep
- Individuality *AND* Unity
- *Frequency*, **Intensity** & Duration

in-Formation Literacy Action Platform™ by Jeffrey V. Kelly, M.A.T.

Information Literacy is: *"The ability to extract, accept, and create good value from needed information."*

Top 10 Barriers to Becoming Information Literate/Action Literate:

10• Information overload/Information noise/Over thinking

9• Cognitive dissonance- difficulty managing conflicting feelings and facts

8• Misplaced emotion and fear of what is true

7• Arrogance/insecurity/jealousy

6• Unaware of biases and relevant phenomographic personal barriers

5• Laziness and impatience

4• Acting upon information that one *wants* to be true but that is not true

3• The inability to reserve judgment when needed/helpful/appropriate

2• Misusing thoughts/prayers/discussions/committees as a cover for inaction

1• Disinformation/Misinformation

Top 3 Ingredients of Action Literacy:

3• Actions are helpful/ethical

2• Actions are performed in a timely manner

1• Action or inaction is based on the understanding of what cannot be acted upon, what can be acted upon and what is helpful to act or not act upon

i-FLAP™ Endorsed by Information Literacy/Action Literacy founder Mr. Paul G. Zurkowski, Esq.
jeffreyvkelly@gmail.com Customize i-FLAP™ for you, your school or organization

Practical IL Criteria/Rubric™ for Teachers/Educators/Supervisors/ Evaluators/Instructors/Trainers/ Leaders...To evaluate/grade any task

"Information is...evaluated and assimilated reinforcing or changing the individual's concept of reality and/or ability to act. As beauty is in the eye of the beholder, so information is in the mind of the user."

— Paul Zurkowski, *Related Paper Number Five*, ERIC p. 1

"Critical thinking is the key that unlocks Information Literacy."

— Jeffrey V. Kelly

"We experience an overabundance of information [information overload] whenever available information exceeds our capacity to evaluate it."

— Paul Zurkowski, *Related Paper Number Five*, ERIC p. 1

Information Literacy Criteria/Rubric™ by Jeffrey V Kelly, M.A.T.

Teacher: _____

Assignment/Product/Task:

Sudent: _____

CATEGORY	5 Excellent	4 Good	3 Average	2 Below Average	1 WHAT?!?!
Accurate/ Authentic	Information is clearly supported by details, evidence & reason and data is factual/authentic at least 90% of the time	Information is supported by details, evidence & reason and data is factual/authentic at least 80% of the time	Information is somewhat supported by details, evidence & reason and data is factual/authentic at least 70% of the time	Information is minimally supported by details, evidence & reason and data is factual/authentic at least 50% of the time	Information is not supported by details, evidence & reason and data is less than 50% accurate/ authentic
Accessible	The whole and parts of the assignment/ product are easily accessible	The whole and parts of the assignment/ product are mostly accessible	About half of the whole and parts of assignment/product are accessible	The whole and parts of the assignment/product are barely accessible	The whole and parts of the assignment/ product are not accessible
Context	Assignment/product shows excellent awareness of the audience &/or purpose &/or setting &/or timeframe	Assignment/product shows good awareness of the audience &/or purpose &/or setting &/or timeframe	Assignment/product shows average awareness of the audience &/or purpose &/or setting &/or timeframe	Assignment/product shows little understanding of the audience &/or purpose &/or setting &/or timeframe	Assignment/product shows no understanding of the audience &/or purpose &/or setting &/or timeframe
Clear	Information/product is presented in a crystal clear manner	Information/product is very clear	Information/product is somewhat clear	Information/product is murky	Nothing about the information/product is clear
Relevant	All of the content is completely related to the assignment	Most of the content is appropriately related to the assignment	More than half of the content is appropriately related to the assignment	Less than half of the content is related to the assignment	Nothing is appropriately related to the assignment
Refined	Assignment/product is 100% complete and has all the important parts and nothing unnecessary	Assignment/product is at least 90% complete has most important parts and few unnecessary parts	Assignment/product is at least 70% complete and needs more refining	Assignment/product needs a significant amount of refining	Assignment not started
Value	The breadth and depth of the assignment/product is as valuable as possible	The breadth and depth of the assignment/product is valuable	The breadth and depth of the assignment/product has average value	The assignment/product has little value	The assignment/product has no value
Good/Goal	The completed assignment/product is excellent and has a very clear goal	The assignment/ product is good and has a clear goal	The assignment/ product is average and has a goal	The assignment/ product is below average and has a goal	The assignment/ product is not good and has no discernable goal
Time/Timely Q: Why does time exist? **A:** To keep everything from happening at once!	The product/ assignment was turned in on time	The product/ assignment was a day late	The product/ assignment was 2 days late	The product/ assignment was 3 days late	The product/assignment was never received or too late to evaluate
Miscellaneous Other criteria for feedback like **Effort** or ?..					

Helpful teacher/leader feedback here (and on the back if necessary):

Chapter Four

Founder Found in Istanbul
After 40 Years in the Wilderness

"More and more of the events and artifacts of human existence are being dealt with in information equivalents, requiring retraining of the whole population."

— Paul Zurkowski, *Related Paper Number Five,* ERIC p. 1

The following updated, fact checked and edited interviews with Paul Zurkowski on his trip to and rediscovery in Istanbul, Turkey for this book, was originally published in the:

Journal of Information Literacy

ISSN 1750-5968

Volume 7 Issue 2
December 2013

pp. 163-167.
http://dx.doi.org/10.11645/7.2.1867

Paul G. Zurkowski: On his trip to the first European Conference on Information Literacy

Jeffrey V. Kelly, Master of Arts in Teaching, author and teacher.

Introduction

The following are excerpts from interviews with information pioneer Paul G. Zurkowski that took place over the course of eleven days from Thursday 17th October until Sunday 27th October, 2013. The interviews were conducted in Washington, DC, and Istanbul, Ephesus and Cappadocia, Turkey, covering North America, Europe and Asia. This interview will also be part of a forthcoming collection of writings being assembled to coincide with the 40th anniversary of Zurkowski founding Information Literacy (IL) to be released in November of 2014. The book's working title is *From 40 Years of Information Literacy into the Future.*

The interviews are presented here in four parts: Before arriving in Istanbul; in Turkey pre-conference; during the conference and post-conference.

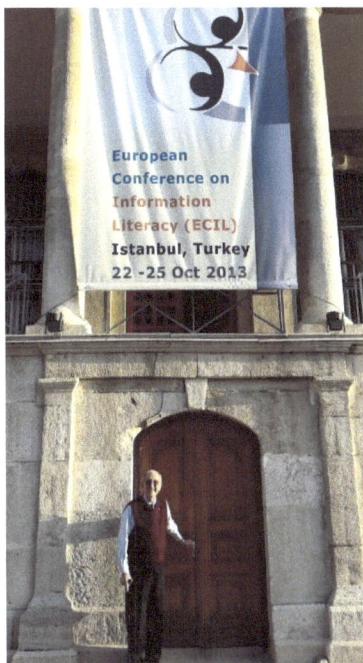

Figure 1: Mr Information Literacy arrives at the ECIL 2013

<u>Before arriving in Istanbul</u>: The following is an excerpt from the first interview on the evening of Thursday 17th October 2013 at Dulles International Airport, Washington, DC while waiting to board a non-stop Turkish Airlines flight that arrived the next day in Istanbul, Turkey, on the afternoon of Friday, 18th October.

Jeff: Thank you Mr Zurkowski for making yourself available for this series of interviews to be conducted as you prepare to open the first European Conference on Information Literacy (ECIL) with your keynote speech in Istanbul five days hence. I couldn't help but notice that your energy level belies a man of 80; where do you get all this energy?

Paul: Well thank you Jeff for documenting this important trip to Turkey. I draw energy from knowing that there will be over 300 information professionals from over 50 countries and 5 continents attending this much anticipated four-day event at the crossroads of Europe and Asia. I am also fortunate to be joined by my wife, Peg and my daughter Pam, who is an award-winning nurse and who will be presenting her poster *Case Studies in Information Literacy for Nurses and Nursing Education* from the University of Pennsylvania, Philadelphia, PA, USA.

Jeff: Are you nervous about your speech?

Paul: No. I enjoy and look forward to speaking to professional groups, especially those with worldwide participation. I have written six versions of this speech trying to hit the right points and in the process have come up with a new title for my speech: *Information Literacy is Dead, Long Live Information Literacy!*

In Turkey pre-conference: The following is an excerpt from another interview that took place during the ECIL pre-conference tour to Ephesus, Turkey on 20th and 21st October:

Figure 3. Pre-ECIL conference tour: Paul Zurkowski; librarians from around the world and friends visit the ruins of the Library of Celsus, one of the largest libraries of the ancient world, in Ephesus, Turkey

Jeff: How did you come up with the phrase, Information Literacy (IL) as used in your letter to the National Commission on Libraries and Information Science, USA while you were president of the Information Industry Association Washington, DC so long ago in 1974?

Paul: The explanation is quite simple. Information industry companies found that once information was produced in machine-readable form, they could deliver it in any medium their customers desired. During the fifth year in the life of the Information Industry Association in 1974, we had grown the membership from about 12 original companies to about 70. I could see these companies' efforts were changing the fundamentals of publishing and that the population as a whole needed to be educated in how to make the fullest possible use of the new services. It just made good sense. So I wrote to the National Commission urging universal IL training. At that stage, well before mobile phones, desktop computers, or any of the technologies we enjoy today, access to these services was tied to mainframe computers, requiring a very specific skill-set of the users. In my upcoming keynote I renew my request for such training, but focus it on teaching elementary school children as you have been doing, a more achievable idea.

During the conference: The following excerpts are from an interview that took place at the Cultural Centre wing of the Harbiye Military Museum in Istanbul, Turkey on Wednesday, 23rd October:

Figure 2. From left: Peg and Paul Zurkowski with daughter Pam Cacchione in the Inner Garden within the Harbiye Military Museum and Cultural Centre at the opening reception after Mr Zurkowski's keynote speech

Jeff: Now that you've been here at the ECIL for a few days, what is your impression of the conference so far?

Paul: I see it as a watershed moment for IL around the world.

Figure 4. Jeffrey V. Kelly, Serap Kurbanoğlu, Paul G. Zurkowski, Maria-Carme Torras, Sonja Špiranec and Pam Zurkowski Cacchione at ECIL 2013

Jeff: What do you think about what Indrajit Banerjee from UNESCO said during his opening speech concerning information *AND* media literacy?

Paul: I wrote about "useful communications media" in my original 1974 paper to the NCLIS. So, I've always known the importance of media; how else can a message get through? It makes sense what you say Jeff that media is simply the way content and meaning are delivered. You cannot have one without the other. Arguing about which is the bigger concept is a waste of time.

Figure 5. Autographs and pictures with Mr. Paul Zurkowski after his successful ECIL keynote on opening night.

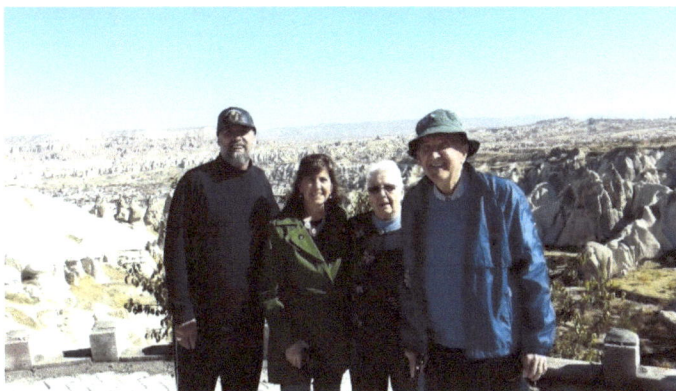

Figure 6. Jeffrey V. Kelly, Pam Cacchione and Peg and Paul Zurkowski developing their "experiential literacy" with nature's vast expanse of "information" all around them in Cappadocia. [Phenomenographically speaking, as ECIL keynote speaker Christine Bruce might say]

Post-conference: The following excerpts are from the interview that took place on the Cappadocia, Turkey, ECIL post-conference tour, 25th & 26th October and while traveling home from Istanbul to Washington, DC on 27th October:

Jeff: Now that the conference is over what are your perspectives?

Paul: The conference for me was like a revelation. At times, I felt like an outsider looking in to this wonderful community that I somehow helped create. Being asked for my autograph and posing for picture after picture was truly humbling for me. A very attentive young volunteer even asked me to sign his conference t-shirt! All the while, I was making friends with many, many informed virtuosi from around the globe.

Jeff: What are some specifics about the conference?

Paul: Co-chairs Serap Kurbanoğlu of the department of information management of Hacettepe University and Sonja Špiranec of the department of information and communication sciences of Zagreb University did a fantastic job dreaming up and putting together this seminal event for IL. I am so glad they found me through my friend and colleague Forest Woody Horton, Jr. and invited me to be here. The facilities worked very well and the conference was a resounding success bringing the informed virtuosi from near and far. A new era of universal IL is sure to follow this wonderful conference as its major landmark contribution.

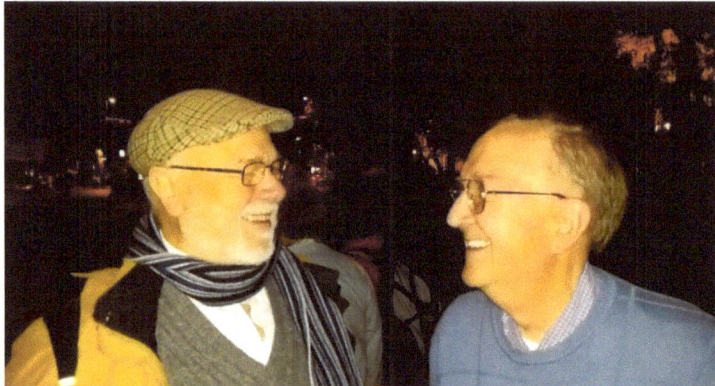

Figure 7. Fast friends: Closing speaker, Ralph Catts and Paul Zurkowski meet for the first time on the streets of Istanbul on the way to Cappadocia. Zurkowski said this picture is indicative of the instant connections he felt meeting people from all over the world during the conference.

Jeff: ECIL highlights?

Paul: There were many but one that comes to mind was when Professor Xiaojuan (Julia) Zhang from Wuhan University, school of information management said to me, "You are well known in China…and we have a lot of people!" She said this during another highlight for me, the workshop I led, *Marketing efforts essential to starting your own information business.* Many participants were interested in starting their own business and may contact Association of Independent Information

Professionals (AIIP) president Jocelyn Sheppard. Other highlights were talking with Albert Boekhorst and attending the presentation by Christine Bruce. I would have liked to attend the talks of so many others. I heard that the talks by Carla Basili, Ralph Catts and Maria-Carme Torras; were very interesting, as were many others.

Jeff: What is next?

Paul: Well, what good is being information literate if the information or wisdom is not used for good? We have many challenges in the next 40 years and the discipline that comes with IL can be at the forefront of making the world a better place. In my keynote speech, I called for a country-by-country effort as a social building block to do what you, Jeff, are doing in your classroom and teach IL in the primary grades by teaching critical thinking. As you put forth in your ECIL presentation, students can start learning IL through critical thinking at around age seven and that laying the foundation for lifelong learning *and* creating can begin from conception with proper nutrition, healthy brain stimulus and appropriate loving experiences, all to help create information-literate world citizens. Searching Google and cutting and pasting alone do not make IL. When I visited your class of 6th graders, I saw how teaching IL through critical thinking is an "open sesame" to these students to the adult world. They are being launched into their lives as my proposal nearly forty years ago, if implemented, would have been doing ever since. The world would be a better place if that had happened.

Also in my keynote, I called for a mapping of the IL universe somewhat like the Human Genome Project. I hope some from the informed virtuosi take this up. Finally, ways must be found to enable ordinary people to produce and wield countervailing power to effectively restrain the harmful forces of economic inequality, media control and disruptive politics challenging the effectiveness of representative governance, using IL as the framework for discourse and action…for good informed

Figure 8. Autographs, fan photos and an exciting but long trip...and yet this IL pioneer arrives home wheeling his own bags...with a smile.

decision making. I called for a "Coalition for Citizen's Information Rights and Responsibilities" a junta organized by librarians, who I see as the informed virtuosi to wrest control of the information switches from the power mongers who are doing damage to representative governance. Honest governance is dying and needs to be given an IV injection from the IV (informed virtuosi). I hope to see more of [them] in Dubrovnik, Croatia, for ECIL 2014. Remember, a future for IL is not inevitable. Long live IL! [Mr Zurkowski was unable to attend 2nd ECIL, Dubrovnik. Ed.]

Acknowledgements

Thank you to the following for providing financial support and encouragement for this project, via Kickstarter: Vivian Malloy; Ted Rowell; David & Barbara Heagy; Father Ron Potts: Christopher M. Kelly; Bill & Marge Walsh; Jocelyn Sheppard; Bruce Becker; Carole D'Achille; Michael Kane; Francis Sullivan; Dolly & John Rasmussen; Paul Phillips, Catherine, Megan and Tom Kelly, Pamela Zurkowski Cacchione; Mary Grace Sloan; Steve Malloy; Vivian Birney; Dr. Ron Redmond; Stephanie McGovern; Marcie Scott; Carol Rollie Flynn; Laura & Matt Fetters, Calvin Lehew and Paul Zurkowski.

"When we first decided to organize the ECIL (European Conference on Information Literacy), we started discussing possible keynote speakers for this initial conference. Paul G. Zurkowski, as the creator of the concept of 'information literacy,' was the first name that came to our minds. However, we had neither the courage nor trace of him to contact him personally."

— Serap Kurbanoğlu

Chapter Five

Information Literacy is Dead…

"It is operationally impossible to separate reality and information."

— Professor Anton Zeilinger, Quantum Information Physicist

"'Literate' comes from 15th century Latin meaning , 'one who knows the letters' and came to mean, 'educated' in reading and writing. Since the beginning of the Information Age, being 'literate' has evolved beyond just reading and writing and is increasingly applied to a growing variety of literacies. Whether media literacy, political literacy, visual literacy, emotional literacy, math literacy, financial literacy…literate is used to mean 'learned' and 'able'. If information is reality, as Professor Zeilinger says, then Information Literacy *is* the all encompassing literacy but arguing among the literacies is a waste of time. As Zurkowski suggested, supporting each other in all the good literacies and mapping the IL universe is a much better use of our time."

— Jeffrey V. Kelly

"…Long live Information Literacy!"

— We the People

INFORMATION LITERACY IS DEAD,
LONG LIVE INFORMATION LITERACY!

KEYNOTE REMARKS OF PAUL G. ZURKOWSKI, Esq.
Founding President of the Information Industry Association, Washington, DC (1969-1989)

FIRST EUROPEAN CONFERENCE ON INFORMATION LITERACY (ECIL), ISTANBUL, TURKEY
TUESDAY, OCTOBER 22, 2013 – 6:00 PM

{Remarks updated for the book: *Zurkowski's 40 Year Information Literacy Movement Fueling the Next 40 Years of Action Literacy.* On the Occasion of the 40th Anniversary of the founding of Information Literacy, November, 2014}

Ladies and Gentlemen,

I'm excited and thrilled to be here.

This conference marks an historic moment for information literacy. I will make this presentation under the new title: *Information Literacy Is Dead...Long Live Information Literacy.*

Information Literacy started out as the logical extension of library literacy dealing primarily with the applying of library skills to emerging mainframe computer search techniques, books, journals, microfilm and microfiche and a growing library of new information services that were the base from which the information age emerged.

It must be noted that at the time of my submission, "The Information Service Environment Relationships and Priorities. Related Paper No. 5" to the National Commission on Libraries and Information Science, Washington, DC in 1974 there was/were:

- no desktop computers (IBM's came out in the early 1980s and the Mac arrived in the mid-80s),
- no Internet and no World Wide Web (www, which arrived in 1989) and
- no mobile/smart phones, laptops, or tablets (all more recent innovations).

Today Information Literacy has become the overarching concept, the core element of lifelong learning, enabling everyone to apply library and information skills and resources to supporting our ability, society's ability, to progressively grow in information, knowledge, understanding and wisdom. So it follows: Information Literacy is dead...long live Information Literacy!

Yes, there was a national purpose to the presentation I made to the Commission in November, 1974. I was pointing out that there was an industry developing enhanced services to increase the quality of life, the profitability of businesses, the missions of charitable groups, the operations of governments, etc. But the world literally had a trained incapacity to use them. They were new and were just being introduced to their respective markets.

My Related Paper No. 5 suggested that by providing universal Information Literacy training the population, the business world and the gross domestic product, reflecting increased efficiency and productivity, would result in increased per capita income. Such universal training would, as well, increase and stimulate the free and open marketplace of ideas, a central guiding policy goal of the industry.

This is still true today. To get the maximum value from all these recent technical advances, universal information literacy training is still needed to realize the full potential of what Information Literacy offers. Searching the Internet alone is not Information Literacy. My friend master teacher Jeff Kelly who is giving a paper at this conference on how he teaches 6th graders Information Literacy through critical thinking demonstrates that fact daily in his Washington DC classroom where most of his students treat their smartphones as human appendages. I've addressed Jeff's classes in the past and have witnessed how his approach is an "open sesame" to his students into the adult world. They are better equipped to enter and be fully functional in it. They are being launched into their lives as my proposal nearly forty years ago, if implemented, would have been doing ever since. Society would be a different and better world if that had happened.

We must as a society be sure the young know these tools are the instruments of Information Literacy, not just entertainment and quick answers to a moment of curiosity, as thrilling as that can be. Taking full advantage of an Internet search is also a special achievement as librarians know. And there are other kinds of research: interviews of experts for their expertise and wisdom, surveys and much, much more. Relying on the searchers wisdom built up over, in some cases, 10,000 hours of information work, in interpreting the results of the research to provide the library patron with as full an understanding of the research results as possible. It is a thrilling life experience each time.

In the final analysis Information Literacy when fully exercised is indeed a work of art.

For my part, 1974 was the fifth year in my service as President of the Information Industry Association. As a "Johnny Appleseed of information", I had spent a large part of those years ferreting out across the country the innovators who were applying the primary rule of the industry: Information, once available in machine readable form, can be custom-delivered to the end user in the users' preferred delivery medium. This was indeed a key new industry literally bursting with new ways of customizing the delivery of whatever is known or knowable to mankind, all worthy of national support. My submission to the Commission was a plea for that support for the industry, for the nation and, today, for the world.

I renew my call, this time, for a worldwide universal program of information literacy training and education starting in the primary grades. I do so with increased urgency since the world is facing new challenges which can be better met if everyone knows what we mean when we say information literacy and can apply it. Put this on your to do list when you return home. Accelerate the process. Society can't afford to let it lie fallow again. Make sure an open marketplace of ideas is a primary value to be achieved.

This conference features presentations on approximately 50 different literacies all within the Information Literacy family itself. Just imagine the effectiveness of this seemingly endless variety of Information Literacies will mean to society over the next 40 years, roughly equal in time to the passage of time since I coined the phrase in 1974. Recognizing these literacies suggests the need for a map of them all that highlights similarities and differences. I suggest that it could follow the genome mapping process that would greatly improve the public's understanding of this amazing development on display here at this conference.

Before going into the details of the vision I have for Information Literacy, let's find out a little about just who is here. We need to get to know each as quickly as possible.

If people from each region could find a gathering place during the Welcome Reception to gather and meet, I would really like to come by so we might recognize each other later in the conference. As your continent or region is called please raise your hand, waive your program or show us how excited you are.

• The Middle East • Africa • Europe • North America, South America, the Caribbean and

Central America • Far East– Asia • Australia and Oceana, ¨• Anyone else who hasn't been heard from?

We are all excited to be here. Let's hear it for IFLA, UNESCO, the Organizing Committee and all who helped get us here. That was great! Thank you.

Part 2 begins now:

When I think of the New Information Literacy I think about what issues we will face over the next 40 years and the role information literacy can play in dealing with them. Obviously we come with many different values and aspirations, histories and cultures; however we all are challenged and united by today's profound economic, social and political changes. Today's world is far different from the world of 1974. However, Information Literacy will help bring us all together in our search for solutions to the problems the world faces. There are common threads of hope and inspiration that will help people take advantage of the opportunities the changing world conditions will provide the courageous people who choose an information literacy career path. It's up to each of us. Like Girl and Boy scouts we need to start thinking about earning our next merit badges.

The challenges the world faces are enormous. So, too, are the opportunities.

Ways must be found to enable ordinary everyday people to produce and wield countervailing power to effectively restrain the disruptive forces of economic disparity and politics challenging the effectiveness of representative democracy.

Just as the information industry operated as an early adapter to changing, political, economic and social conditions by taking technological advances in stride to lay the groundwork for the Internet and the World Wide Web, the Information Literacy movement can operate as an early adapter to the changing conditions we all now face worldwide. The new situation we face calls for motivating and guiding citizens in using Information Literacy and critical thinking disciplines to help mobilize citizen-based Direct Democracy efforts to respond to the challenges representative democracy faces today in contending with outside power sources seeking control over governance ideally intended to serve everyone.

The history of the world is replete with historical events illustrating that whoever controls the switches of information exercises that power for temporal good or evil. The imbalance of power we live with today has to be addressed democratically.

The first Chairman of the Board of the Information Industry Association board was William Tyndale Knox. His family traces its history back to the time of Henry VIII and the advent of the printing press. There is a William Tyndale Knox in every generation of Knoxes since Henry the VIII's time. In at least two generations they were women. The Knox family honors the memory of William Tyndale, an innovator who brought the Gutenberg Press to England. He saw it as a revolutionary invention to provide information to the people. Henry VIII had prohibited the printing of an English Language Bible. Tyndale went to the continent to print such a bible. Henry VIII's forces ran Tyndale to the ground, had him strangled and burnt at the stake as a heretic demonstrating how serious the crown was about the control of the switches of information.

The power of the Church to sell indulgences fell victim to the power of printing when the Church, in need of raising funds, called on Gutenberg to print hundreds of copies of the 43 line indulgence form normally hand lettered in Greek by Monks. The printed form left a space for the sinner's name and a monk's signature. It immediately became a temporal rather than an eternal document. Printing many copies of the form took away the eternal touch of the indulgence practice to the extent that Martin Luther included indulgence forms in his reformation efforts.

The American Colonies experienced the colonization practices of English Crown involving the first newspaper published in North America, the Boston Newsletter. It operated under a Crown Copyright, a device giving the King of England power over what could be published. When the Boston Newsletter supported independence for the colonies, the King took away its "right to make copies" as a seditious newspaper. That incident led the framers of the Constitution to create a new set of rules for patents and copyrights in Article I of the US Constitution. It gives ownership to the products of the mind to authors and inventors. It was one of the primary motivations for the colonists to seek independence from the Crown.

What we are seeing today is the effects of a similar power play. Witness the current events that have resulted in almost a complete loss of power for the American people over their government. It's hard for us to imagine the American people favoring the closing down of the government. But events have conspired to give a small minority the power to do so.

The wealthy were freed by the Supreme Court to express their opinions through unlimited rights to donate money to political campaigns. They get their views known and written into the law as a result. A current case before the court seeks to eliminate any limits on political donations; the current limitation is $120,000 per election apparently not enough to "own a member of Congress." With no total limit on donations, the wealthy could pay for the whole campaign and increase their power in the legislature. Where is the equal treatment before the law in that arrangement?

Political parties use the census figures every ten years to carve out safe election districts giving incumbents safe reelection relieving them of being responsible to their constituents, the people. The fact is that both parties do it

The media have failed representative democracy through partisan abuse of the public airwaves largely by casting issues as a contest, avoiding full disclosure of what is involved in the issues and just reporting who is ahead at the moment. They are controlling the political process by removing the substance from public discourse and converting major issues to simple scorekeeping entertainment.

These events have reinforced the perception that citizens have no impact on the process. With no hope of affecting the system, many voters give up and do not vote.

These examples are serious challenges to representative democracy and at the same time offer librarians with a history of motivating citizen participation in governmental affairs and elections through the support for and the application of information literacy.

Information Literacy with an emphasis on direct democracy offers a way for society to right the ship and deal with the glitches that have developed in representative democracy.

My plan involves:

• an active role for Information Literacy in the area of direct democracy, an extension of the role librarians have always played.

• creating citizen's *Action Literacy* coalitions based at libraries around the world.

• an operating plan for implementing an approach to issues we as a civilization will face over the next 40 years.

Here is how the plan could work.

The library community has been the watchdog in the past in privacy matters over the use of library patron borrowing records and other issues. Now that some powers that be have decided their full commitment to the public for library services is no longer needed because "everything is right there on the Internet," information literacy gives the library community the opportunity to transition itself to serve the same public with the library skills, training and respect for information in a new way. Information Literacy is a necessary element for assuring equal treatment before the law.

I have been working to:

• develop a step by step procedures manual to outline what resources would be needed, how they would be applied, what library resources and citizen participation is needed;

• to create *Action Literacy* coalitions to lead, community by community, state by state, country by country, to the development of the rules of the information road that lies ahead. When the automobile was invented rules of the road had to be developed. A function of the Coalition is to monitor the rules developed for information. Rules are being established without any watch dog organization to verify whether the proposed rules are good, bad or indifferent. We need better than that;

• to create a manual to address the fact that there is no established process to engage citizens in issues like Information Rights and Responsibilities and Information Policy or for that matter simply how to become a non-partisan force on any and all issues arising today. Political assassinations such as those of President Jack Kennedy and his Attorney General brother Bobbie Kennedy, limit how many talented people are willing to risk their lives in elected government service. Where are they? Are they any less interested in how a country is governed? Can they become involved in and support coalition efforts outside of the political party system? All guided by Information Literacy.

I find this four step process: information becomes knowledge, knowledge becomes understanding, and understanding becomes wisdom helpful in explaining to the general public what information literacy means in a general way and how it can serve their interests.

Ben Franklin and his Society for Useful Knowledge
Provides a precedent
For Information Rights and Responsibilities

The organizing principals of my plan are based on a system created by Benjamin Franklin in about 1730 and a system he sustained throughout his lifetime. He called it The Society for Useful Knowledge. Mr. Franklin's driving force was based on the fact that the Colonies were populated principally by farmers and merchants and were purposefully limited by the Crown in how much freedom they had. They needed useful knowledge just to get through the day.

Within The Society for Useful Knowledge, Franklin organized what he called the Leather Apron Committees, community groups of 12 people, later nicknamed the Junta, (meaning together) to explore what society's needs were and how to address those needs. Each one of the 12 was given the task by Franklin of writing a short description of a specific problem of their choosing needing to be addressed. Ben wrote several such statements to prime the pump. The Junta would once a month retire to a pub in the evening to discuss their approach to each issue. It may even have been one of those papers that suggested the study of lightening to Ben. It is known that they later dispatched a junta member to explain electricity and the need for lightning rods on buildings throughout the mid-Atlantic colonies. When more colonists sought to join Franklin's Junta, Franklin refused to expand it beyond 12 for practical reasons and recommended to newcomers that they form their own Juntas.

Implementing such a plan today would require a body overseeing the work of the Juntas as a parent organization. In my plan it would be the *Action Literacy Coalition.* Election to the ALC would provide an academy of people committed to overseeing the process to develop competent and recognized policy statements designed to give participating citizens a clear understanding of the issues and a certainty as to the accuracy and value of ALC publications the fact that "All politics is local" means that under this plan, each area, each library, each community organization, would be encouraged to create a Junta to work on community interests in their geographic area or their area of interest. It would fall to the Coalition to publish the papers, emulating the early colonists "Pamphleteers" which helped set up the American revolution. Their publication would go viral on the social media if we did our job right.

In the process the *Action Literacy Coalition* would help we the people and would provide a pathway for citizen involvement in the country's civic affairs.. The most important part of this process is the need for information literacy skills, fact checking and where necessary text editing. Everyone needs an editor. Libraries and other Coalition organization members would be looked to in fostering Juntas, each of which would develop information relevant to the issues they were addressed. Some information would come from existing sources, other information would be developed by study of sources of information, by observation and by interviewing the experts and surveying public concerns and attitudes. The Coalition could distribute other publicly available information serving the cause.

It is interesting to note that the Library of Congress supports House and Senate Members with its Congressional Research Service. Members of both houses can ask for help in understanding legislative proposals or for help in drafting or analyzing new legislation. This is a confidential service. Only the member can divulge what CRS came up with in response to a Congressional office request. It is a service just like the support that Librarians and others could provide to a local Junta. Their studies would be evaluated by members of the Coalition, individuals inducted into an *Action Literacy Coalition* to assure the studies were fair, non-political, and factual all leading to informed public understanding of the issues involved. This would create a shared wisdom in the community needed in addressing specific issues.

See the book "The Society of Useful Knowledge" by Jonathon Lyons, Bloomberg Press, New York, 2013 for the complete story and the Colonial setting that fostered its growth and development.

The role of Libraries within the *Action Literacy Coalition* program would be central and vital. A variety of other organizations would be welcome as well.

I have met with Kathleen Teaze, Director of the Prince George's County's Memorial Library System, Maryland, USA. I enjoy knowing her and her take on Information Literacy and other issues. She is interested in the Coalition idea. She is willing to help beta test this program in the Prince George's County Memorial Library System.

Some librarians are leaving libraries to create their own businesses. The president of the Association of Independent Information Professionals compared the association's membership to a virtual library system without the brick and mortar based on their previous library experience and practices. The Association of Independent Information Professionals, a global association of some 400 such firms serving businesses and other organizations in need of professional information searching skills and the understanding and wisdom earned in many years of library services. The *Action Literacy*

Coalition will work with these companies as participants in the Coalition. This will also draw in the information industry firms with information resources of vital importance to such efforts. The AIIP already has negotiated wholesale data base search costs for its members. Junta members seeking research on their topics would have recourse to local AIIP members as well as libraries. The AIIP has been a big help to me in preparing for the "Marketing Aspects of Starting Your Own Information Company" workshop scheduled for Thursday from 1:30 to 3:00 pm. Please be advised that you must pre-register for the workshops to enable the committee to have a meeting room suitable for the number of advance registrants.

The text of an earlier version of this presentation that appears in the publication of Conference presentations and addresses the steps the Information Industry provided its members in building a 950 member organization that are relevant to the work of the proposed Coalition.

In conclusion, it should be clear there is a world of opportunity to be conquered by skillful people in many roles, but the most important is the one regarding the care, feeding and the extension of Information Literacy. Long Live Information Literacy.

I am interested in staying in touch with all of you about these ideas in the hopes of extending the concept around the world. I'm looking forward to working with everyone in this area of human endeavor.

Please send me an email your reactions to, questions about or suggestions for the idea contained in this presentation. That will plug you into the Information Literacy and *Action Literacy* movement.

Addendum – What good would it be

Here is a list of the good things possible with an active Coalition:

- Publication of the results of the mobilization of the *Action Literacy Coalitions*. Create electronic linkages with as many participants as possible.
- Identify the steps to empower people to live enriched public and private lives - creating new employment opportunities by recognizing new markets for information services as well as Information Literacy services.
- Enhance quality of life for citizens through active participation among friends. Enlarge and enhance the meaning of volunteer service.
- Attend to Citizen Information Rights and Responsibilities, issue by issue.
- Develop and support routes to effective and rewarding citizen participation in policy and governance issues outside the party system.
- Provide a perpetual early warning system for monitoring the practices in the financial field known to have endangered worldwide economies.
- Engage the media to promote the routes facilitating citizen participation
- Provide an opportunity for meaningful application of Lifelong learning through civic participation
- Promote citizen use of critical thinking
- Like my teacher friend Jeff Kelly, teach Information Literacy skills through critical thinking in elementary schools and up.
- Develop apps to assist students in developing Information Literacy skills and understanding.
- Seek out volunteer leaders and impresarios to make ALCs real and exciting for all.
- Engage unemployed and partially employed citizens in their own rescue through the application of Information Literacy tools to generate new wealth-generating work opportunities.
- Engage the professions, the arts, educators, attorneys, etc.
- Anticipate the end of work by developing a new sense of what work is.

End

Chapter Six

Staying Ahead of the Curve

"We, the people of the world, face awful crises arising in large measure from the control of information, a control in turn arising from the inability of citizens to navigate the super abundance of information that comes into their perception, while at the same time other interests are perfecting information techniques including disinformation, to disable citizens in order to achieve their self-serving goals regardless of the dangers to civilization."

— Paul Zurkowski, from an early draft of his AIIP Keynote Speech, Baltimore, Maryland USA, April 2014

"Information Literacy and lifelong learning are...self-motivating, self-directed and...self-empowering, which means that they are aimed at helping people of all age groups, genders, races, religions, ethnic groups, and national origins, no matter what their social or economic status may be, or role and place in their communities or society in general."

— Dr. F. Woody Horton, Jr. *Understanding Information Literacy: A Primer*

Edited by the Information Society Division, Communication and Information Sector, UNESCO *Information for All* Programme, Paris, France 2007 p. 2-3

For more from Dr. Horton:
http://infolit.org/unescos-overview-of-information-literacy-resources-worldwide-2nd-ed-2014-2015/

Staying Ahead of the Curve

Prepared Remarks Keynote Speech

Paul G. Zurkowski, Esq.

At the 28th Annual Conference of the
Association of Independent Information Professionals (AIIP)

Hyatt Regency Hotel, Baltimore, Maryland

April 4, 2014

I am delighted to be here with you today. It's been a treat for me to work with Jocelyn and Jan in preparing for today and to discover what we at the Information Industry Association (IIA) originally called the Information on Demand companies have grown into. Sue Rugge, Haines Gaffner, Andy Garvin and Maureen Malone, who is with us today and lives near me in College Park, Maryland, all are contemporaries of Roger Summit and Carlos Cuadra as active members of the Information Industry Association formed in January 1969. They all participated in the creation of the association working out relationships for themselves, among the publishers, hardware companies, database owners and distributors, niche publishers and entrepreneurs working to make sense of information content as a business. Forerunners of meetings like yours here today crowd into my mind and I see them all here with us today, as you push forward building your businesses with enthusiasm and excitement, experiencing the growth and maturity coming from you efforts. Know how important you are.

I am here to share ideas about how you can capitalize on your opportunities and leverage your assets to increase your business. That mutual goal will be pursued by thinking a little outside the box exploring business initiatives that will keep you ahead of the curve.

I will talk about a silent crisis facing everyone in the world today. Secondly, I will describe a new initiative called the Information Action Coalition to extend Information Literacy into the homes, factories, offices - everywhere. We will explore together the roles that Independent Information Professionals play in working with and through the Information Action Coalition. Get excited.

The Silent Crisis.

What is the silent crisis facing everyone in the world today? The Washington Post answered that question last Sunday when it carried an op-ed piece entitled "Are we heading for the fall of democracy?" Its author is Stein Ringen, an emeritus professor at Oxford University in England. He cited the fact that Greece invented democracy and enjoyed 250 years of success. "But when privilege, corruption and mismanagement took hold the lights (of Democracy) went out," he said.

Ringen cites the fact that Britain's past two governments "came up against concentrations of economic power that have proven politically unmanageable."

And America, Ringen says, faces a link between inequality and inability to act that is on sharp display. "Power has been sucked out of the constitutional system" he wrote, "usurped by actors such as political action committees (PACs), think tanks, media and lobby organizations."

"In Athens," he concluded, "democracy disintegrated when the rich grew super-rich, refused to play by the rules and undermined the established system of government. This is the point that the United States and Britain have reached."

Information overload contributes to the disruption of democracy underlying this crisis for We the People of the world.

The fact is more and more information is a double-edged sword. Yes, it helps us solve problems if we know how to navigate it. If we don't, it leaves us open to the control of information by others who have the resources and purpose to confuse, distract and overwhelm our best efforts. For many, apathy follows. That result needs to be addressed if the crisis is to be solved.

Whoever controls the switches of information rules and controls how issues are articulated and resolved.

When the history of the last score of years of the 20th century is written it will be recorded that the Information Industry changed the world. Now Information Literacy must help the world change. The alternative has already been shown to be a disaster.

A little history on how events have gotten me started on this campaign.

Last year, the organizers of the First European Information Literacy Conference in Istanbul Turkey invited me to give its keynote address in October. It drew 362 attendees from 59 countries. The US was well represented. I was invited because in 1974, 40 years ago this November, I defined and conceptualized Information Literacy in a proposal to the National Commission on Libraries and Information Services. I submitted it in the fifth year of my efforts to know and bring into the Association all the people in what we called the Information Industry. It was obvious we were creating a whole new industry that the world had never seen. The industry was creating products and services for which people had a trained incapacity to use. Action was needed to train them in the use of these emerging products. The Internet some 15 years later, picked up on my message and also defined the Information Service Environment. Back then I did not realize that the Information Service Environment was different from the Reading Services Environment. My proposal is a historic document because it describes the industry at that time including who these companies were and what services they offered in what media. I have provided a copy to AIIP where you can access it.

In preparing for that keynote in Istanbul, I became quite excited about Information Literacy all over again. I got reacquainted with the massive effort the library world has devoted to developing the details of what Information Literacy is today.

In preparing for that keynote I discovered that there is a historic precedent for both the information industry and Information Literacy in a general sense buried deep in American history. In the early 1700's Ben Franklin created the Society for Useful Knowledge as a way of dealing with the scarcity of "how to" information in the isolated colonies. The work of the Society Franklin created was done by the "Leather Apron Committees," made up of small businesses, craftsmen, of all kinds, the sort of people clad for practical purposes in leather aprons. They were forerunners of both the information industry and information literates of their day. Franklin laid on each of the committee members the task of writing about a problem they faced in the colonies without anyone to turn to for "how to" answers.

The Leather Aprons met at local pubs monthly to discuss the papers. This practice spawned the pamphleteers. That and the deteriorating relations with Great Britain led to the revolution.

What Ben did with the Society was the equivalent of today's Information Literacy movement. The big difference was Ben was addressing information scarcity. Today's Information Literacy movement seeks to create a new "Era of Enlightenment" by teaching curious citizens Information Literacy skills to take advantage of the huge resources that can become information overload, by knowing how to navigate through it to find answers, just the opposite problem to the one Franklin addressed.

So I suggested in my speech in Istanbul that what was needed was a modern day Ben Franklin's Society for Useful Knowledge.

I have been working on the details of such a system ever since. The factors that makes this a critically important step for the world's 21st century are the corruption and undermining of democracy and the perfected disinformation efforts disrupting thoughtful consideration of the alternatives societies face, to the point that citizens end up believing the wrong information and vote against their own self-interests, or drop out of the democratic process entirely.

The objective of the Information Action Coalition is to engage people with a social conscience to get involved in and support efforts to empower average citizens to navigate through information overload problems and get the answers empowering them in the vital matters of their lives and their country. Isn't that your objective as well?

The Information Action Coalition will produce, test and guide efforts to:

1.) Create a template that can be used to introduce citizens nationwide to the benefits of Information Literacy and to work together with the public libraries, AIIP and others to begin training citizens in the art of Information Literacy and its transforming ability to add clarity to life.

2.) Pair up the Readers Service Environment of the library world with the Information Services Environment created and sustained by the information industry to encompass the modern problem solving ability of Information Literacy;

3.) Create an operating plan where Libraries and private companies can work together to engage as much of the population as possible in realizing the real benefits of Information Literacy in their lives and to provide training so to do.

The plan ultimately calls for the creation of a Global Network of Local Organizations to address information overload's impact on society and to take the lead in creating a new Era of Enlightenment by extending Information Literacy to curious citizens who are frustrated by today's information overloaded realities.

I hope you with your significant library experience you will agree and will be interested in exploring the ways this IAC can address the crises while enhancing the financial prospects of your businesses.

Libraries offer the logical first strategic partner for the effort. There are over 3100 counties or equivalents in the United States with local public libraries providing more coverage of the population of the United States than the cell phone ads all claim.

There are many opportunities for AIIP members to get involved to capitalize on all the action this will stimulate. You are also the logical ones to support the effort with the broad library experience so evident in your membership and the entrepreneurship needed for your businesses to thrive.

Information Literacy is the compass for navigating today's information overload.

The initial step is to create a Beta Test with the following steps:

Identify four sample seminar topics – such as Caregiving and Rudiments of Information Literacy including expert speakers like Jeff Kelly who teaches critical thinking and Information Literacy to 3-12 students in Washington, DC. Jeff also spoke at the Istanbul Conference last October.

Design and hold the seminars – up to 2 hours in length, just enough time to demonstrate the role of Information Literacy on a topic of broad interest. Each subject would have two seminars dedicated to that subject designed to attract the same people to both events, and to observe what the seminars achieved. Promote the seminars to the public hoping to draw 20-25 citizens to each one. It will also be necessary to document how these Seminars are managed to provide guidance for future efforts.

Find ways to involve Libraries in providing Information Literacy Training for Beginners, Intermediate and Expert. This might involve developing working relations with universities, retired educators, book clubs, AIIP and more future coalition members.

Create opportunities within the Library to benefit from the experience of AIIP members with Information Literacy practices and the publicity and selling techniques acquired by making their businesses appealing to the public. Entrepreunrial business experience is critical to the success of the effort and we may find libraries interested in teaming up with you former librarians with business experience in a fair and supportive way.

Video tape the seminars to give management needed information about how to make seminars successful in introducing citizens to Information Literacy.

In my discussions with the CEO of the Prince George's County Memorial Library System, Kathleen Teaze, who is working with us to develop the beta test of these ideas, has been welcoming of the idea to offer an opportunity specifically to AIIP members right from the start to actively work with the Libraries on ways to promote the service to the community in a business like way, possibly as a one or two day per week office hours for AIIP members at the library to act as an advisor to citizens frustrated by information overload. During down time, the Agent would be free to work at their business on the cell phone and in interviews of their clients or outside resources and do research in the library. Research employees and private sector participants could contract to perform research projects for citizens at a standard discounted quasi pro bono rate, encouraging private sector participation and avoiding unfair competition complaints. I have been told libraries are ready to offer new services rather than just stand in the door greeting patrons with "Welcome, what can we do for you today?"

Operating manuals will be created to assure fairness in the management of these activities in the county, across the country and around the world.

A gazillion other steps will be needed: Setting up a U.S. 501c3 non- profit organization, developing a communications effort, publicizing and promoting the seminar approach, finding the leadership to run the program across the country and developing a superior fund-raising effort, to name the more obvious needs.

This plan offers a systematic way to combine experienced members of public libraries with the experienced information entrepreneurs in AIIP in a coordinated way to as rapidly as possible create an enlarged number of citizens working to overcome the information overload problems standing in the way of society being able to deal with our crisis issues.

How does a program of this nature affect you and your bottom line?

The text of my remarks has a little less than a page of business ideas flushed out by this discussion of Information Action Coalition and its action plans. But I want to hear from you.

This is the time for Questions and Answers: In a turnabout here are my questions for you:

What did you hear that suggested there was a business opportunity for your kind of business. I'll assume you want to keep your best ideas to yourself if you don't speak up. Do you think we have these crises? Are they information crises for the world? Will an Information Literacy campaign help? What business do you see yourself doing in the middle of all this? What else should we do? Is your business guided by a sense of justice? Are you an organizer, as I feel I am? What are your answers?

Business Opportunity notes for AIIP members:

It gives you a slant on businesses today: It's not business as usual; it requires you to think through what business opportunities are opened to you and your assets based on your out of the box knowledge of how the information service environment works.

Learning corporations. Talk with corporate Human Resources folks. You could build a business helping businesses understand the information age and what it takes to operate in this new age. How more information oriented employees could help the business involved.

Information Action Agents – co-workers with Librarians through Action Literacy Coalition efforts at supporting public libraries. Local sponsors could fund these activities.

Contract with Libraries to (1) provide Information Literacy training (good place to find future employees), (2) to help with recruiting for library activities in the Information Services Environment.

Providing Library employees short course training on the entrepreneurial approach to library services. This will involve educating the governmental funding units that set the budgets for libraries. Training seminars tailored to the entrepreneurial needs of expanding library services to overcome information overload could be directed at county-wide library systems.

Caregivers could be the focus of one of the planned ALC Demonstration seminars. It begs for the implementation of a catalog of local, county by county services to overcome the overload fog that frustrates first time caregivers. Collating abstracts of relevant articles on Caregiver resources or other topics selected for seminar treatment would be especially valuable in support of Information Literacy efforts to break the information overload logjam facing new caregivers. For experts in the field, sponsored conferences on such subjects as caregivers offer sometimes paid speaking opportunities which also contribute to the recognition of your firm's expertise.

There is no pathway to participation in governance, other than political parties, for citizens cracking the overload code. Information services keyed to citizens entering the participation process would be essential. For example, newspapers provide day to day calendars of scheduled hearings on legislation which serve the lobbyists who are thoroughly briefed on the legislation involved. There is no tracking service starting from the day bills are introduced so that individual taxpayers can get a grip on the effect of the proposed legislation. Citations to Legislative histories and to the introduction and explanation of bills covered by Congressional Information Services could become a specialty of Independent Information Professionals as the program extends across the country.

And one for AIIP itself: A service of the AIC might be regular information product and services brain storming sessions to alert members to the needs emerging from the efforts addressing information overloads. Such products arise in the natural course of events within the information service environment.

In the light of our discussion Government contracting may be a valuable course offering for AIIP.

The clue to marketing is the identification of the organizations emerging to serve a class of new participants in each issue's natural constituencies.

Conclusion:

First and foremost: We, the people of the world, face awful crises arising in large measure from the control of information, a control in turn arising from the inability of citizens to navigate the super abundance of information that they face, while at the same time other interests are perfecting information techniques including disinformation, to disable citizens in order to achieve their self-serving goals regardless of the dangers to civilization.

Information Literacy is an antidote to information control exercised by the special interests.

Now is the time to combine public library and private sector experts to put in play a program of introducing citizens to the power of Information Literacy to resist attempts to intimidate and control them and to empower them as citizens to making democracy and their lives work.

It's a wonderful world when you are involved in it as I saw at last night's reception.

Before closing I thank all you rock stars of AIIP for participating and your organizing committee for inviting me to speak with you today. It is memorable occasion for me.

Finally let me say once more: The Information Industry changed the world. Now Information Literacy must help the world change. Know how important you are!

Chapter Seven

The New Era of Enlightenment

"Whoever controls the switches of information, rules and controls how the issues are articulated and resolved."

— Paul Zurkowski, LILAC Spring 2014 Video Address

"The principal of freedom of expression, should apply to past, present and future forms of media [the medium for how content is delivered], including the Internet. Our insistence on the plural form of Knowledge Societies rests on the conviction that there is no single uniform model, dictated by technology or market relations, to which all societies must conform. The nature of Knowledge Societies should be conceived as plural, variable and open to choice, and freedom of expression is inseparable from this vision."

— Indrajit Banerjee, Director, Knowledge Societies Division, Communication and Information Sector, UNESCO, Speaking points for the 17th Session of the Commission on Science and Technology for Development, 14 May 2014, Palais des Nations, Geneva, Switzerland, p. 5

Information Literacy and
The New Era of Enlightenment
Paul G. Zurkowski, Esq.
Founder: Information Action Coalition

Prepared Remarks Video Address for the 10th Anniversary *Librarians' Information Literacy Annual Conference* (LILAC 2014), Organized by the Chartered Institute of Library and Information Professionals' (CILIP) Information Literacy Group (IL Group), UK, 23rd-25th April, Sheffield Hallam University, Sheffield, South Yorkshire, England

It is an honor and a privilege to participate in this 10th LILAC 2014. I am excited and pumpedup about it. The results of LILAC's steady flow of state-of-the-art accomplishments in Information Literacy are stunning. They lay the ground work for what I propose. Congratulations to you all. Be excited about your future inside Information Literacy.

Here are three things I will talk about with you.

I will tell you how I came to propose universal Information Literacy training in 1974 to the U.S. National Commission on Libraries and Information Science.

Then you may be shocked to learn how an emeritus Oxford University professor describes asilent crisis threatening the democratic countries today.

Finally we'll talk about how this crisis offers Information Literacy a central role supporting democracy. By doing the things it is capable of for mankind, Information Literacy will create a new Era of Enlightenment.

Here is how Information Literacy came to be involved in the flow of the history in the early days of the information age in 1974.

The Information Industry Association (IIA) was created at a Philadelphia meeting ofinformation industry executives in November 1968 roughly at the birth of the information age.

Prior to that time no one seemed to know or care about such an age. But here was a business community staking out the Information Age as its own mostly because no one knew what aninformation product or an information industry was.

Credit IIA with pushing the envelope to define what it meant and what itdid.

I entered the field when I met some key members of IIA's founding group of company executives while serving as a legislative assistant to U. S. Congressman Robert W. Kastenmeier. He chairedthe Copyright Subcommittee of the House Judiciary Committee which was considering the first revision of the 1909 Copyright Act in half a century. The information industry executives were interested in whether input into a computer was a copyright infringement. They knew that whatever the answer was it would weigh heavily on their developing businesses.

I was hired in December 1968 as President of the IIA and my first priority was to grow its membership. As I traveled around the country seeking people engaged in the information business, I became the Johnny Appleseed of the information business. Wherever I spoke informationcompanies sprung up. By 1989 the IIA had grown to 950 members.

Five years into its life IIA members were discovering that workers in their markets literally hada trained incapacity to use their products. They knew how to use printed abstract journals butnot databases with the same information which required skilled searching of mainframe computers tofind answers. My proposal to NCLIS explained the New Information Service Environment IIA was creating information services requiring user training in how to do mainframe computer searching ofdatabases. Users needed to have information skills, which I called Information Literacy.

As the IIA grew it became something of an arbiter on Information Policy issues. We successfully opposed the Government Printing Office proposal to produce all government documents in 50x reduction ratio microfiche. Our members overcame objections of some European PTTs (Postal Telegraph and Telecommunication) to an invasion of American databases, to name just a couple ways the industry was laying the groundwork for the Internet and what followed.

With the advent of the Internet it was clear that the need that gave rise to the words Information Literacy, basically the need to train people in the searching of mainframe computers, was pretty much resolved by the Internet wave. So that original "brand" of Information Literacy is not as large an issue today; However, Long Live Information Literacy in the Internet Age and beyond.

That's when all of you pitched in and carried us forward to where we are now.

The Silent Crisis; "Are we heading for the fall of Democracy?"

The Washington Post newspaper on March 23, 2014, carried an op-ed piece asking just that question: It was by Stein Ringen, an emeritus Professor at Oxford University. He cited the fact that the Greeks, noted for creating Democracy had enjoyed 250 years of its success.

"But when privilege, corruption and mismanagement took hold in Greece, the light [of Democracy] went out," he said.

He said Britain's past two governments "came up against concentrations of economic power that have proven politically unmanageable."

As to America, Ringen stated, "It faces a link between inequality and inability to act that is on sharp display. Power has been sucked out of the constitutional system and usurped by actors such as political action committees (PACs), think tanks, media and lobby organizations."

"In Athens, he concluded, "Democracy disintegrated when the rich grew super-rich, refused to play by the rules and undermined the established system of government. This is the point that the United States and Britain have reached today."

Similar stories on other issues have identified the trend creating this crisis: Increase the power of the mighty and decrease the power of everyone else.

Information overload can contribute to this disruption of democracy.

Ironically the fact is that more and more information becomes a double edged sword. Information helps solve problems if we know how to navigate the information overload. If we don't know how to navigate, it leaves us open to the control of vital information by others who have the resources and purpose to confuse, distract and overwhelm the citizenry's best efforts. For many discouragement and frustration disable them and apathy follows.

Whoever controls the switches of information rules and controls how the issues are articulated and resolved. In history there are many examples of how information controls have been used: William Tyndale published the first English Bible against the prohibition of Henry VIII and paid for that heresy with his life. He was captured, tried, convicted and strangled before being burned at the stake

Information Literacy has the power to create a new "Era of Enlightenment." Information Literacy skills are the key to taking advantage of our huge information resources, sometimes referred to as our Information Overload. People can be taught how to navigate through the overload to find answers to their problems.

Information Literacy training based on the training in library and school courses would provide the course content to launch the enlightenment program. It in turn, will empower average citizens to navigate information resources to get the answers empowering them in the vital matters of their lives and their countries.

What does the next 40 years hold for Information Literacy?

This global movement must now turn its attention to the application of Information Literacy skills in homes, offices, schools, factories, and governments everywhere. This will enable democratic forces to deal with the corruption and undermining of democracies. Disinformation efforts disrupting citizen consideration of the alternatives policies will be reduced in their power. By providing good information citizens won't be confused into voting against their best interests.

This then is a call to action to the Information Literacy advocates, experts, librarians, educators and information businesses to focus on extending the Information Literacy training on the universal basis I first suggested in 1974.

Information Literacy can empower average citizens to navigate through the information overload problems and get the answers empowering them in the vital matters of their lives and countries.

I am working on a global plan to engage members of the public around the world in a program of Information Literacy demonstration projects. This will provide citizens Information Literacy experiences with follow up activities to encourage them to seek more complete training. It is called the Information Action Coalition. It seeks to create a global network of local organizations to support coalition members in extending universal Information Literacy Training. It is worldwide in its intent and perspective. I say again the magic words, A Global Network of Local Organizations, not a national network, not a U. S. network and definitely not a command center. The whole world stands at the door step of a New Era of Enlightenment. The Information Action Coalition is designed to provide the means for all of us involved to coordinate our efforts and to learn from the experience of local organizations at home and in other lands.

My vision is that your CILIP Information Literacy Group, for example, with your sophisticated capabilities has an essential role to play in sharing the lessons it has developed and learned with Information Action Coalition members. That would help shape, apply experience to and move the ball forward for Information Literacy. Groups like your IL Group and LILAC do a great job moving everyone by providing sheet music that common-minded people can easily follow. We have to figure out what will work best in the UK, Europe, and around the globe.

The Information Action Coalition plan is in beta test in my home county in Maryland. The Prince Georges County Memorial Library System Director is working with us on the beta test. The Coalition is also exploring with Prince George's County Economic Development agency the economic development prospects of this Information Literacy initiative for its job-creating potential. Such an economic thrust can cover costs of merging library efforts with private sector marketing efforts. One proposal calls for the creation of a truly public/private Think Tank in select libraries to provide thorough and fair reports to assist citizens to involve themselves in the complex issues of our times. The U. S. Library of Congress offers similar services to Members of Congress through its Legislative Reference Service.

There are 3,100 counties in the US with public library systems as a possible broad geographic foundation for the U. S. nation-wide Information Literacy training program. Funding for research projects would be sought from businesses, foundations, government and other traditional sources. Membership in the Coalition would support the administrative costs of the Coalition through membership fees.

The Information Action Coalition has adopted the following simple formula to suggest its goals:
Learn to read, then read to learn;
Learn to search, then search to learn
to Live Sustainably Free.

The Information Industry by creating the Information Service Environment has changed the world. Now a universal Information Literacy training program can help the world change through creating a New Era of Enlightenment.

A Video Presentation to the 10th LILAC 2014
April 23, 2014 by
Paul G. Zurkowski, Esq.,
Founding President of the Information Industry Association 1969-1989
On the occasion of the
40th Anniversary Year of the Founding of Information Literacy

Chapter Eight

Action Literacy — The Next 40 Years

"The global Information Literacy movement must now turn its attention to the application of Information Literacy skills in homes, offices, schools, factories, and governments."

— Paul Zurkowski, South Dakota Keynote Prepared Remarks, October 2, 2014.

"Government should not perform services for its citizens which the citizens are capable of performing themselves."

— Paul Zurkowski, *Related Paper Number Five*, ERIC p. 26

"...Zurkowski launched a movement that for 40 years has spread throughout the increasingly complex information industry and the world's library science, information science and broader academic communities and is now driving Action Literacy into everyday life around the globe, where more and more people and organizations are empowering their lives using the ideas and skills contained in this book to access, create and take ethical action upon good information."

— Jeffrey V. Kelly, *Action Literacy*, p.1

Action Literacy:

Key to Success for We the People

In the Information Age

Prepared Keynote Remarks of

Paul G. Zurkowski, Esq.

at the

South Dakota Library Association Convention, Pierre, SD USA

October 2, 2014

It is an honor and a privilege to participate with you in this South Dakota Library conference. Your web site says you have held annual meetings since 1919 except for the war year 1945. That would make this the 95th annual conference representing a long and illustrious record of involvement with the people and their well-being in the great state of South Dakota. I thank Danielle Loftus for the idea of inviting me here, based on her experience at the First European Conference on Information Literacy held in Istanbul last October where I also spoke.

Public libraries are the key to continued evolution of Information Literacy and to developing the new age of discovery based on what we are calling Action Literacy, for the worksite and lifelong learning purposes.

My objective today is to encourage an exchange of ideas growing out of my original vision of Information Literacy and its continuing relevance to the economic, political and social changes of the 21st Century. To date Information Literacy efforts have emphasized academic versions of Information Literacy rather than real-life, take action, actionliteracy.

I have three ideas to share with you. I will tell you how I came to describe the new Information Service Environment being created by the Information Industry in the 1970s and 1980s and to propose universal Information Literacy training in 1974 to the U. S. National Commission on Libraries and Information Science (NCLIS).

Then I will share with you an Oxford professors concern about the silent crisis threatening democracies today.

Finally we'll talk about how the crises the world faces offer libraries and Information Literacy a central role in shaping the future of America and the world.

1. How did Information Literacy come to be involved in the flow of the history of the information age in the early days?

The need for it was created by the launch of a new industry in 1969. The Information Industry Association (IIA) was born at a Philadelphia meeting of information industry executives in November 1968 to which I was invited and did attend.

Here then came a business community staking out the Information Age as its own because so few knew what an information product or an information industry was. The industry explained information by what it did and by creating a whole new information service environment in the process.

I entered the field when I met some key members of the Association's founding board while serving as a legislative assistant to U. S. Congressman Robert W. Kastenmeier (Wis.). He chaired the Copyright Subcommittee of the House Judiciary Committee considering the first major revision of the 1909 US Copyright Act in half a century.

A month after the founding meeting of the Association in December 1968, I was hired as president of the IIA. My first priority was to grow its membership. By 1989 the IIA had grown to nearly 1,000 members, not just content companies but companies engaged in all aspects of the Information Age. IIA functioned more like a community development company than a narrowly focused trade group.

By 1974, five years into the life of the association, some members were discovering workers in their niche markets literally had a trained incapacity to use their new products. They knew how to use ink print materials but not databases with similar information requiring computer search skills.

My 1974 proposal to NCLIS explained that the then emerging Information Service Environment was producing information services requiring user training in how to do main frame computer searching. Users needed to have information skills, which I called Information Literacy.

NCLIS ignored my proposal as being too far ahead of the times. Only a small population of early adopters had to figure out how to do it. For the most part they worked in many largely niche markets in a wide array of professions. In any case, they were being taught how to do it by the companies supplying them new media information services. Available only on mainframe computers

Laptop computers were still ten years away. The IBM desktop reached the market early in the 1980's; the Apple Macintosh appeared in 1987. The World Wide Web that brought the Internet to the masses, showed up in 1989. Smartphones, i-Phones, tablets, Google, eBay and Amazon, the Cable systems and the rest came even later.

With growing access to the Internet it was clear that the need that gave rise early to the Information Literacy movement, basically the need to train people in the searching of mainframe computers, was pretty much resolved by the Internet wave. It may seem that that first generation "brand" of Information Literacy is not as prominent an issue today. But the fact of the matter is that current Internet experience proves that there still is a need for the development of search skills. Without this new step for Information Literacy which we are calling Action Literacy, what most casual searchers are getting is only "spot" or "look-up" information to trivia-type questions, not in-depth research or problems solving answers.

2. The Silent Crisis; "Are we heading for the fall of Democracy?"

The Sunday Washington Post in March of this year carried an op-ed piece asking just that question: "Are we heading for the fall of democracy?" It was written by Stein Ringen, an emeritus professor at Oxford University.

He cited the fact that the Greeks, noted for creating Democracy, had enjoyed 250 years of its success.

"But when privilege, corruption and mismanagement took hold in Greece, the light [of Democracy] went out," he said.

He noted that, "Britain's past two governments have come up against concentrations of economic power that have proven politically unmanageable."

As to America, Ringen stated, "It faces a link between inequality and inability to act that is on sharp display. Power has been sucked out of the constitutional system and usurped by actors such as political action committees (PACs), partisan think tanks, media and lobby organizations."

"In Athens," he concluded, "democracy disintegrated when the rich grew super-rich, refused to play by the rules and undermined the established system of government. This is the point that the United States and Britain have reached."

A corollary is offered by Economist Joseph Stiglitz who won the 2001 Noble Memorial Prize in Economic Sciences by pointing out that while economic theory is based on all sides utilizing perfect information, in fact there is no such thing as perfect information. Some people have more power and their interests inform the prevailing economic theories. This is called Information Asymmetry. This imbalance results in the inequality currently corrupting the American economy and its Democracy.

We here together have a challenge and the means to address it. Action Literacy has the power to answer the question, "Who controls the switches of information?" with "We the People." Who else but the people know how to address this underlying problem?

In history there are many examples of how information controls have been used:

William Tyndale published the first English Bible against the prohibition of Henry VIII who was worried he'd lose control of the new Church of England if people for the first time could actually read the Bible in their native language. Tyndale paid for that heresy with his life. He was burned at the stake as a heretic. The first Board Chairman of the IIA was a man named William T. Knox. His family goes back to Henry VIII in England. Every generation of Knoxes had a William Tyndale Knox, at least two of which were women, honoring his memory. No wonder I discovered the question who controls the switches of information.

The first newspaper in the Colonies was the Boston Newsletter that published under a Crown Copyright. When the Newsletter supported the American Revolution, the Newsletter became, in the eyes of the Crown, a seditious newspaper and it lost its Crown Copyright and was shut down. That incident is responsible for the copyright and patent provisions in Article 1 of the U. S. Constitution granting ownership of the products of the mind, not to the Sovereign, but to inventors and authors. That approach exemplified why they fought the revolution. Freedom of speech, press, and religion were left for the later Bill of Rights.

3. What does the next 40 years hold for Information Literacy?

The Information Literacy movement must now turn its attention to the application of Information Literacy skills in homes, offices, schools, factories, and governments. This will enable democratic forces to deal with the corruption and undermining of democracies. Disinformation efforts disrupting citizen consideration of the alternatives policies will be reduced in their power. Democracy will be refreshed and citizens empowered. When citizens can access good information they won't be confused into voting against their self-interests.

This then is a call to action by Information Literacy advocates, experts, librarians, educators and information businesses to focus on extending Information Literacy training on the universal basis I first suggested in 1974.

That brings us to the plan a committee of six in Prince George's County has been working on for the past year.

In the long run it is a global plan to engage members of the public around the world in a program of universal Information Literacy training projects. The focal point of the effort is Public Libraries. This will provide citizen Information Literacy training and experiences with follow up activities provided by Public Library research staffs.

We have yet to agree on a name. For our purposes today let's refer to it as the Action Literacy Coalition. It is intended to be a coalition of a variety of players with similar concerns organized in a global network of local organizations to support coalition members in extending Universal Information Literacy Training. It depends for its success on the independence and absolute political neutrality of Public Libraries. Action Literacy Training will have no political activity. What action citizens take with the knowledge and understanding they derive from Action Literacy Training will be theirs alone to take. The Action Literacy Coalition will be as perfectly apolitical and neutral as the Public Libraries we will work with.

It is worldwide in its intent and perspective. The whole world stands at the doorstep of a New Era of Information Discovery that now follows the opening of the Americas. The world is round. Patterns of thought were broken and discoveries of all sorts followed.

Action Literacy Coalition is being designed to provide the means for all of us involved to coordinate our efforts, to develop local **Action Literacy Training Events** and provide a website through which to share the experience and forward thrust of local organizations at home and around the world.

We have been working with Kathleen Teaze, Director of the Prince George's Memorial Public Library System in my home county in Maryland.

Here is her slant on it:

"Librarians know," she says, "that we can't just stand in the front doorway anymore welcoming patrons by saying: Welcome. Thanks for coming. What can we do for you today?" Today, she offers an example of a new welcome: "Can we show you how the new 3-D printer system works?"

She knows libraries today have to have an active and enriched outreach to the public to get members of the public involved through services of the library in all aspects of their lives.

She has been a tower of strength in our deliberations constantly reminding us of the new resources and services available in public libraries.

She gets it. She sees Information Literacy training as the bedrock of library community outreach programs. She is a driving force in designing a workable system that libraries around the world can use to extend a kind of "just in time" understanding and use of Information Literacy skills to break through the information overload to divulge problem-solving information to the man and woman in the street.

She notes that it is better to teach people how to fish then to try to supply the fish they need to live.

So, there you are: Libraries playing a major role in the lives of people and nations.

We can learn a major lesson from the approach of information technology companies to the market place.

Today's technology companies work to address key problems every human being has and to provide solutions for what might be called their kitchen table kind of issues. We all are the customers these companies serve. We all face issues these companies are addressing for us. That's their business plan and it is the basis for the fact that one of their number is now the largest U.S. company. When they say they are building the Next Big Thing they are saying they have identified the next big problem for people and they have a fix for it. And we buy into it and discover new things and approaches in the process.

Have you ever thought of libraries as participating in our times in these terms?

The Action Literacy Coalition recognizes its purpose is to serve exactly that same market – people with problems. We think Action Literacy Training, with library support, can make Action Literacy the Next Big Thing by demonstrating a capability to address the kitchen table kinds of issues we all face. Its first job will be to introduce the public to the Information Literacy process of digging deep enough in the search process to reach the "Ah-ha!" moment of finding the answer to their problem. Then they will know what Information Literacy means to them and they will be more effective as human beings and civic members of society.

They will know the race belongs not to the swift but to the Action Literate.

The plan we are beta-testing called **Action Literacy Training Events** addresses, for example, how Caregivers, when first faced with that responsibility, can find the information necessary to guide the decisions they must make. Action Literacy will lead them to computer sources, to physical centers for caregiver support services, to printed and other sources in a growing field of caregiver information. Action Literacy will introduce them to the back up services libraries offer to the public introducing non-digital natives to state of the art ways of finding and accessing information they need to know to make caregiver decisions.

Each Action Literacy Training event under the plan would be in the range of 2 hours in length and will take place in a public library supported by local speakers and library research staff. Coalition members may provide sponsorship support. In the Beta test we are looking for 20-30 participants. Videos would provide "flip-the-classroom" techniques to introduce the Action Literacy concept which includes due diligence and critical thinking elements sent to participants in advance to make best use of the 2 hour training sessions. Adults learn best through interaction with their peers. Some events will have follow-up sessions to determine the impact of what participants have learned.

The plan includes an administrative support activity including running a vital website for the program and a fund-raising effort to generate financial support for library services beyond their present budget. New York Public is exceptional in that it generates donated funds equal to the city and state funds in their budget. That 50-50 split is a real national goal we will be able to support as the program grows especially given the opportunity Action Literacy offers for both work site and lifelong learning services provided through libraries.

There are over 3,000 counties in the USA with public library systems as a possible broad geographic foundation for this version of the nation-wide universal Information Literacy training program I recommended to NCLIS in 1974.

The U. S. Library of Congress offers customized Legislative Literacy support in drafting and preparing bills for submission for members of Congress through its Legislative Reference Service.

The Information Industry created the Information Service Environment which today continues to bring almost daily changes to everyone's life. Now a universal Information Literacy training program can help the world adapt to these changes. For me, my experience helping the information industry evolve the Information Service Environment is one bookend of my professional career and working to engage that service environment in a new era of Information Age Discovery through Action Literacy with the library community is the other bookend.

We all know the devil is in the details and that in researching a problem you must get more deeply into those details than a spot information "look-up" keyword search produces. Google and other search engines can get you deeply into issues but you need good skills at formulating the search questions so your search addresses the variables inherent in the problem you are addressing. A spot information "look-up" query often produces 100,000 or more citations. Obviously, to find the best in-depth answer you need a more carefully crafted query. We are developing language for this process that will ring true for people once they experience the Eureka joy, the "Ah-ha!," the "I have found it" moment.

For those who experience those Eureka moments Action Literacy indeed will become the "Next Big Thing" in their lives.

This is the power of Action Literacy Training.

We expect that individuals will experience their Eureka moment as Archimedes did. He is credited with shouting "Eureka!" when he discovered a way to measure the purity of gold, a 14 carat event, to be sure. Today people will have their moment of discovery while digging into the details of their problem. They will need due diligence to be sure their search is complete, accurate and timely.

They will also need critical thinking to assess or measure the "purity" of the answer they found. One of our committee members, Jeffrey Kelly, has taught 6th graders Information Literacy via his Information Literacy Action Platform. The class, as I witnessed it several times, provided the students an open sesame experience revealing how the informed decision-making process works for them.

ACTION Literacy goes beyond database and literature searches, the early domains of academic Information Literacy. This year's LILAC Literature Search of Information Literacy Research projects concluded that the brand of literacy taught in schools, essentially adding substance to doing better individual research, does not translate effectively to the work site. In the corporate world, people need to work with the people who have created the corporate knowledge base. This involves a new skill set to the academic Information Literacy skill set.

As we work with Action Literacy issues we are likely to find other areas where the information literate executive needs to think "outside the box." Outside the traditional Information Literacy "box" means looking beyond the Internet to other sources such as your neighbor who successfully solved the problem you are facing; to a directory of trade associations which was my starting place at the Information Industry Association when I needed to know how other businesses were addressing the problems information companies were encountering.

For the curious the world today is a wild and wonderful place because of the multiplicity of available information sources. I'm sure every research librarian has discovered many such insights and is ready to share them with people with Action Literacy on their minds. Action literacy offers an expanding horizon for us all.

Action Literacy encompasses such other literacies as digital, media and the many other specialized literacies, such as Financial Literacy. It demystifies the whole process. We are all seeking to tap into all sources and by all means fair to enrich, preserve and enhance human experience. This is our duty and our opportunity. If this is not done, everyone's life will continue to be degraded.

How would the Literacy Training sessions work? Let me list a few topics for the Action Literacy training sessions we have in mind for introducing people to Action Literacy.

Critical Thinking. A slogan of the 1930s was "Don't believe everything you see in the newspapers." The same sentiment applies to what you find on the Internet. This event would engage people in understanding how to cross-reference whatever they found. Search as needed and evaluate each finding and learn how to find more efficiently. Libraries would offer participants reinforcing further training in critical thinking.

Action Literacy, Academic and Job Site Information Literacy. Beginner and advanced sessions illustrating similarities and differences in approach to skills, and the bag of tricks for searching the Internet with out-reach to other sources.

Private Enterprise opportunities and risks. In the current recession this event would attract the out-of-work, young people interested in job opportunities and would involve local business among others.

Information Asymmetry as a cause of inequality. 2001 Nobel Prize awarded to Economist Stiglitz who proved economists analyze economy on the assumption that everyone has access to "perfect information" whereas, Stiglitz pointed out perfect information does not exist. Information asymmetry enables disinformation to mislead voters. Information Asymmetry is a major reason for Economic inequality. Asymmetry shunts power to one side of an issue. Action Literacy is its antidote.

How to utilize eBay for fun and profit. It's more complicated than it looks as you find out when you try your hand at it.

The need to create a pathway to citizen civic participation.

Opportunities for Action Literacy Coalition members in the news media, including TV and radio.

Other Action Literacy Training event topics include:

- Professional Performances Get the Job: Job seeking, resume writing, job interview techniques.

- Up to date (using social media) organizational skills.

- Skillful Retirement planning

- Financial Literacy for families and small businesses

- Humane Society animal care skills

- Community needs as viewed by elected representatives – future civic action for citizens

The Action Literacy opportunities know no limit, given the vast opportunity to engage citizens about Kitchen Table issues. Each session starts with introducing Action Literacy in terms they can understand – designed around the problems they face.

The goal I set in 1974 of universal Information Literacy training can be met one problem area for library patrons at a time. Each new problem is special to a different set of people. Each offers an opportunity to reach out to a new group of citizens.

Each library will naturally develop specialties so that within one county's public libraries a wide range of subjects can be addressed to involve local county residents and businesses. Prince George's County has 19 member Libraries. Participating county residents will become familiar with library locations, talented staff, local speakers and their work, applicable resources and policies. They will also find and make new life-long, like-minded friends. With an Action Literacy web site that shares the news of progress, libraries will have access to the enriching experience of events run in other areas that facilitate the creation of duplicate events but with local variations and improvements.

Hot topics will go viral and project first local power, then regional and ultimately national power affecting the fair functioning of Democracy.

This effort created, like so many new technologies, in the inventors' imaginary "Garage." This one is attached to the Prince George's County Memorial Public Library and Action Literacy proponents.

We are interested in your reaction to this outline of the plan and would welcome your participation in developing it further for your own brand of Action Literacy.

South Dakota and Action Literacy: Let's figure out how to make Action Literacy happen here.

Are there any questions?

Thank you all for coming.

Long Live the Library Outreach and Action Literacy.

Appendix

"Consider the source! The original source!"

—Unknown

"Obsession with perfection is enemy to the good"

— Concept attributed to various sources

"Well, what good is being Action Literate if
the actions are not used for good?"

— Jeffrey V Kelly, inspired by Paul Zurkowski

ED 100 391   IR 001 493

AUTHOR   Zurkowski, Paul G.
TITLE   The Information Service Environment Relationships and
                Priorities. Related Paper No. 5.
INSTITUTION   National Commission on Libraries and Information
                Science, Washington, D.C. National Program for
                Library and Information Services.
REPORT NO   NCLIS-NPLIS-5
PUB DATE   Nov 74
NOTE   30p.

EDRS PRICE   MF-$0.75 HC-$1.85 PLUS POSTAGE
DESCRIPTORS   *Data Bases; Federal Programs; *Information Needs;
                *Information Services; Information Sources;
                Information Systems; Library Automation; Library
                Cooperation; National Programs; Professional
                Education; Program Evaluation; *Publishing
                Industry
IDENTIFIERS   Information Industry; *Information Literacy; National
                Commission Libraries Information Science; National
                Program for Library and Information Ser

ABSTRACT
        The relations of the National Program for Library and
Information Services to information literacy and the information
industry are discussed. Private sector information resources are
identified in several categories. The traditional relations of
libraries and with the information industry are described, and
examples are given of situations where traditional roles of libraries
and private sector information activities are in transition. It is
suggested that the top priority of the National Commission on
Libraries and Information Science should be directed toward
establishing a major national program to achieve universal
information literacy by 1984. (PF)

NATIONAL COMMISSION ON LIBRARIES AND INFORMATION SCIENCE
NATIONAL PROGRAM ON LIBRARY
AND INFORMATION SERVICES

RELATED PAPER
NUMBER FIVE

THE INFORMATION SERVICE ENVIRONMENT
RELATIONSHIPS AND PRIORITIES

U S DEPARTMENT OF HEALTH
EDUCATION & WELFARE
NATIONAL INSTITUTE OF
EDUCATION
THIS DOCUMENT HAS BEEN REPRO
DUCED EXACTLY AS RECEIVED FROM
THE PERSON OR ORGANIZATION ORIGIN
ATING IT POINTS OF VIEW OR OPINIONS
STATED DO NOT NECESSARILY REPRE
SENTOFFICIAL NATIONAL INSTITUTE OF
EDUCATION POSITION OR POLICY

PAUL G. ZURKOWSKI

PRESIDENT
INFORMATION INDUSTRY ASSOCIATION

This paper (1) identifies various categories of private sector
information resources; (2) identifies categories of industry/
library relations of a traditional nature; (3) identifies examples
of situations where traditional roles of libraries and private
sector information activities are in transition and (4) suggests
priorities for implementation of the National Program to facilitate
the recognition and maintenance of the mutually supportive roles
of industry and libraries.

NOVEMBER, 1974

The views expressed are those of the author and do not necessarily
reflect the position or policy of the NCLIS. Though related to the
Commission's National Program, papers in this series are not an
integral part of the National Program Document.

Zurkowski Original page 12

TABLE OF CONTENTS

Zurkowski Original page :}

THE GOAL: ACHIEVING INFORMATION LITERACY

Information is not knowledge; it is concepts or ideas which enter a person's field of perception, are evaluated and assimilated reinforcing or changing the individual's concept of reality and/or ability to act. As beauty is in the eye of the beholder, so information is in the mind of the user.

We experience an overabundance of information whenever available information exceeds our capacity to evaluate it. This is a universal condition today for three reasons:

(1) The information seeking procedures of individuals are different at different times for different purposes.

(2) A multiplicity of access routes and sources have arisen in response to this kaleidoseopic approach people take to fulfilling their information needs. These are poorly understood and vastly underutilized.

(3) More and more of the events and artifacts of human existance are being dealt with in information equivalents, requiring retraining of the whole population.

The infrastructure supporting our information service environment transcends traditional libraries, publishers and schools. It embraces the totality of explicit physical means, formal and informal, for communicating concepts and ideas.[1]

---

[1] Including but not limited to telephone, television, radio, human voice and action, newspapers, magazines, books, paperbacks, movies, theater, graffitti, pamphlets, maps, tours, audio tapes, schools, door-to-door salesmen, direct mail advertising, computer data bases, newsletters, microfiche collections, drugstore book and magazine racks, government

From amongst these activities, information publishing activities, whether publicly or privately funded,[2] can be identified as those devoted to anticipating information interests, filtering information abundance and directing ideas and concepts to specific fields of perception in cost-effective and useful communications media.

Such an information publishing activity can be viewed as a prism. It gathers "light" (ideas and concepts) and performs a variety of "refractory" functions (editing, redacting, printing, microfilming, encoding, arranging, etc.). It produces a spectrum of information products, services and systems designed to correspond to the kaliedoscopic needs of the field of users it purposfully selects to serve. The individual user has many facets and shows different needs to the information sources at different times for different purposes.

Anticipating these changing needs and packaging concepts and ideas to meet them is a major evolving economic activity. (See Figure I). This differs from traditional publishing in significant ways which will be discussed later. (See Figure 2).

Figure I demonstrates that information publishing activities gather data of interest to a specific subject, field or market, produce information

---

pamphlets, bookstores, libraries, political campaigns, churches, social clubs, satellite communications, cable television, other broad band communications, cocktail parties, town criers, committees of correspondence, pamphleteers, museums, expositions, etc. Most importantly, however, the infrastructure also includes all of the human skills necessary to the functioning of these physical means, as well as the wide variety of economic structure on which their continued viability depends.

[2] The Information Industry Association (I.I.A.) was established in 1968 and is made up today of more than 70 member companies. The I.I.A. is limited by its charter to commercially chartered, for-profit companies, but the functions of the industry are also performed by non-profit and government agencies. See also Encyclopedia of Library and Information Science, Vol. II Marcel Dekker, Inc., New York, 1974, p. 483 et seq.

FIGURE I

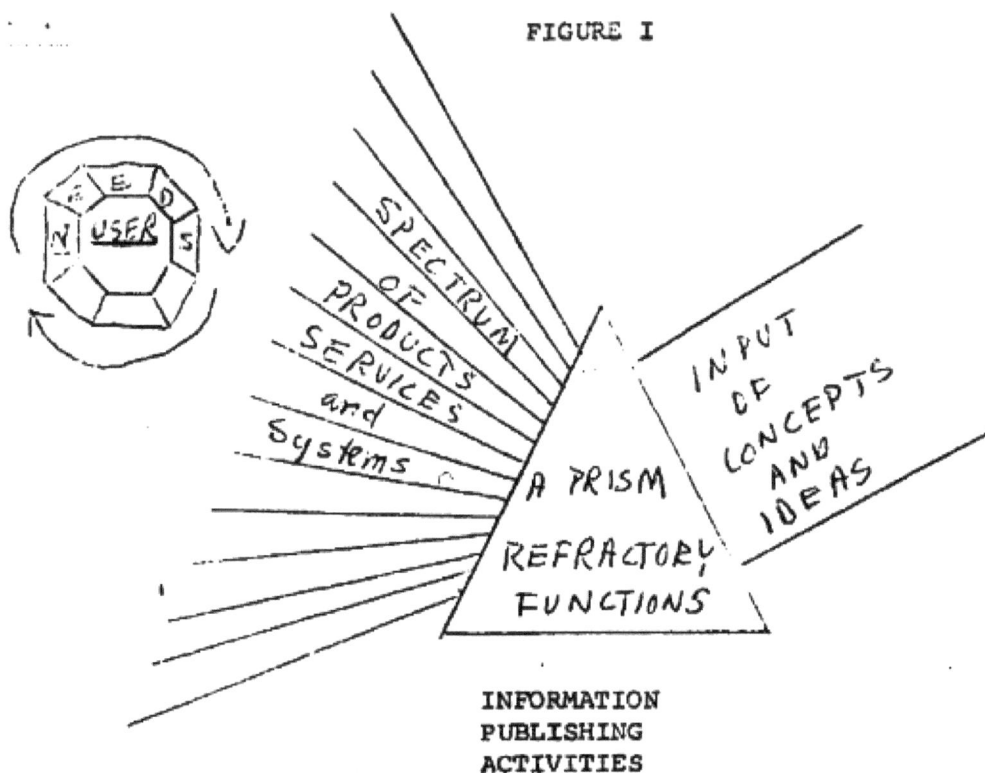

INFORMATION
PUBLISHING
ACTIVITIES

These include:

A. Information Generation: 1. Original authoring or writing (e.g.,
NY Times); 2. Compilation (e.g., Dunn and Bradstreet, R.R. Bowker;
3. Recruitment of authors (e.g. Alfred Knopf); and 4. Cataloging, abstracting, and indexing (e.g., any "secondary service" publisher, like Congressional Information Service or H. W. Wilson).

B. Information Publishing: 1. Editing (all of the above); 2. Formating for original publication (all of the above); 3. Formating for re-
publication in another form (e.g., CIS Microfiche Library; The Readers Guide
Bantam Books; Lockheed on-line system); 4. Distribution (e.g., Richard
Abel; Lockheed; McNaughton Library Service); and 5. Publicizing, marketing,
and educating (all of the above).

C. Technology Applications: ("Hardware"): can be applied in the pursuit of any of the above functions; these include such things as dictating
machine, microfilm camera or reader, computer composition microwave transmission, printing press, computer storage and retrieval optical character
recognition, etc.

Originally page 3 ERIC

Originally page 3 Zurkowski

FIGURE 2

A Book

INPUT OF IDEAS AND CONCEPTS

TRADITIONAL PUBLISHING ACTIVITIES

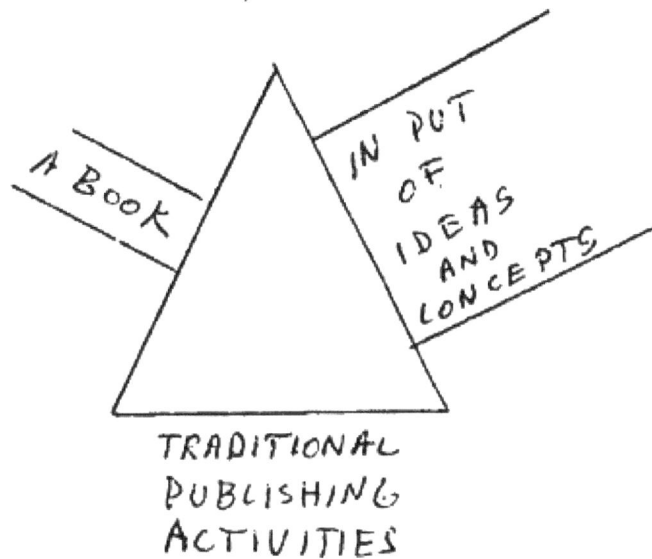

A traditional publisher considers each book an economic entity stand-ing alone. The publisher is successful to the extent that more books suc-ceed than fail. In traditional publishing, the related, parallel portions of the spectrum of products and services which can be derived from the in-put of ideas and concepts may or may not be recognized and may or may not be marketed.

Originally page 4 ERIC

(products, services or systems capable of informing) and focus the information on the intended users expected needs. All of these are labor intensive, intellectually disciplined, costly, risky and capital intensive activities. Their success is measured by the feed-back received from the user.

In a vital marketplace of ideas information publishing activities must enjoy not only the right to succeed but also the right to fail.

In the competitive information marketplace the measure of success is whether a particular enterprise proves to be profitable. The marriage of the profit motive to the distribution information is the single most important development in the information field since Carnegie began endowing libraries with funds to make information in books and journals more widely available to the public.

Since no one can have a monopoly on ideas and concepts (copyright grants only a limited monopoly in a particular statement of ideas or concepts), competition is keen in identifying ideas and concepts with a high degree of relevance to a particular market or group of users and in bringing these ideas and concepts into the field of perception of that market. If the right decisions are made about (a) the identification of ideas and concepts (b) their documentation or packaging, (c) the intended group of users and (d) pricing, the enterprise will thrive and be profitable. If not, it will fail.

"Precisely because business can make a profit, it must run the risk of loss. The strongest argument for "private enterprise" is not the function of profit. The strongest argument is the function of loss. Because of it business is the most adaptable and the most flexible of institutions around. It is the one that has a clear, even though limited, performance test. It is the one that has a yardstick".3/

3/ Age of Discontinuity - Peter F. Drucker; Harper & Row, 1969, p. 237 et seq.

In the government sector no such yardstick exists. Information activities are funded as a value of society. This is a more general standard and one more subject to the laws of inertia.

"One can argue that this or that obselete hospital is really needed in the community or that it will one day again be needed. One can argue that even the poorest university is better than none. The alumni or the community always has a "moral duty" to save 'dear old Siwash'.

"The consumer, however, is unsentimental. It leaves him singularly unmoved to be told that he has a duty to buy the product of a company because it has been around a long time. The consumer always asks: 'And what will the product do for me tomorrow?' If the answer is 'Nothing' he will see its manufacturer disappear without the slightest regret." 4/ Thus, for the user, there is a specific yardstick. Information has value in direct proportion to the control it provides him over what he is and what he can become.

The user is willing to pay for services which enhance his control. Not everyone perceives this as a measure of the value of information. Many who are conscious of the need for information still feel that information, like air, is a free good.

People trained in the application of information resources to their work can be called information literates. They have learned techniques and skills for utilizing the wide range of information tools as well as primary sources in molding information solutions to their problems.

The individuals in the remaining portion of the population, while literate in the sense that they can read and write, do not have a measure for t value of information, do not have an ability to mold information to their needs, and realistically must be considered to be information illiterates.

Figure 3 illustrates the relatively small percentage of people who have attained some degree of information literacy.

4/ The Age of Discontinuity, op. cit.

FIGURE 3

PERCEIVED
VALUE OF INFORMATION

MEDICAL, GOVERNMENTAL
BUSINESS, SCI/TECH
INFORMATION LITERATES

U. S. POPULATION

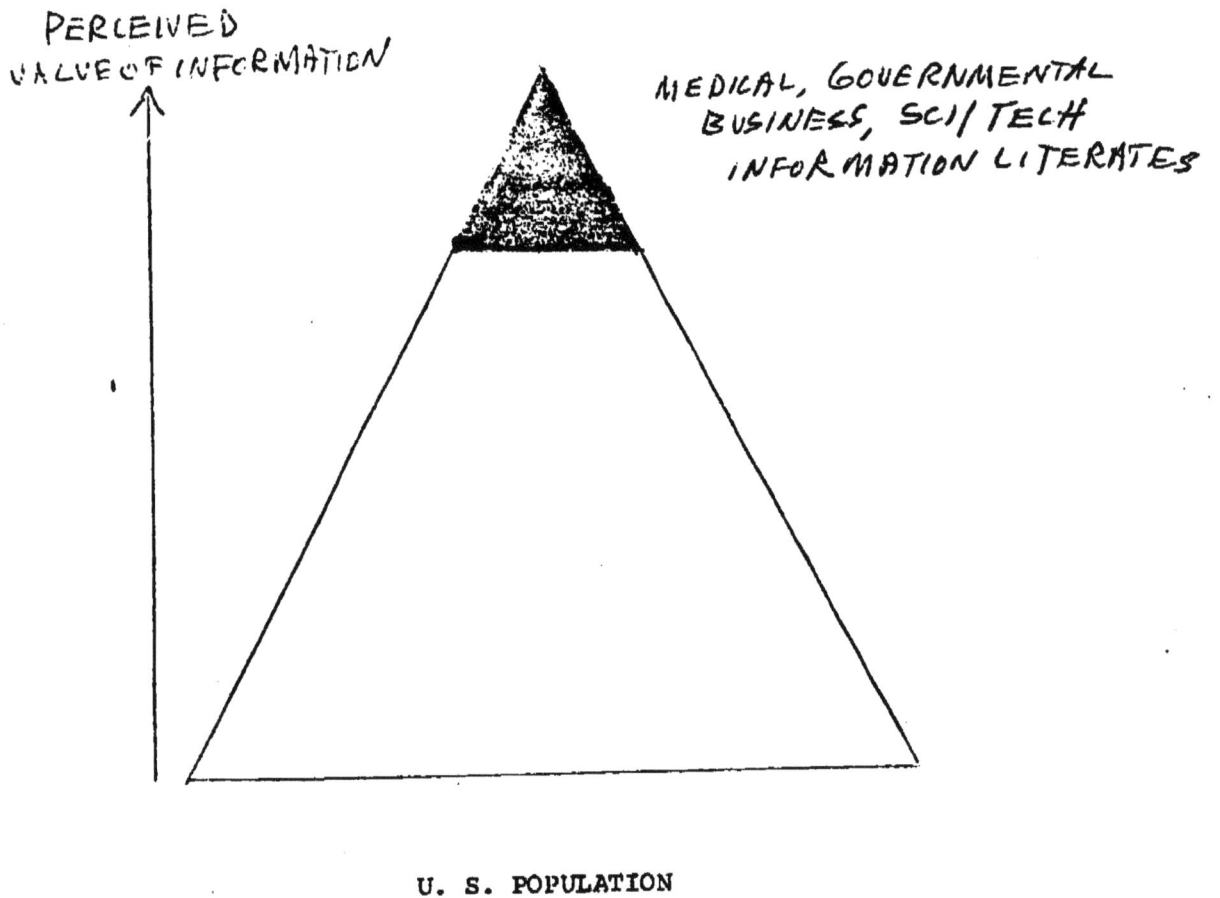

While the population of the U.S. today is nearly 100% literate, only a small portion - perhaps one-sixth, could be characterized as information literates.

The work of the Commission should be viewed in terms of achieving total information literacy for the nation.

This paper seeks to:

(1) Provide indicators of the broad range of services already being offered by non-government, non-library-based business firms.

(2) Identify the policy questions that need to be resolved in order to maximize the pluralistic structure of the information economy already in place in order to achieve information literacy for our entire population, and

(3) Suggest priorities which the commission should consider in attaining the goal of information literacy.

II - PRIVATE SECTOR INFORMATION RESOURCES

A snapshot of the private sector information resources needs to be taken with an extremely wide angle lens. Having taken the picture it is fairly easy to identify and define categories of services, subject areas covered, and, in some cases, even the intended markets for particular products. Specific categories will be identified and examples cited for each without any expectation that the list will be complete.

It must be noted, however, that each resource cited is but one of a group in a spectrum of services offered by a particular company and its competitors and that for each resource cited there exists, in various stages of development, another spectrum of comparable, related or competitive services (cf Figure 1.).

A. INFORMATION BANKS

The creation of an information bank - a resource people can draw on, is a most capital intensive activity.

The Library of Congress MARC program is one example.

Others include:

Shepard's Citations - used in law libraries and by individual law firms, based on the arrangement of legal citations to previously decided court cases.

Science Citation Index and Social Science Citation Index [5] used in research libraries and by individuals, based on an organization of scientific citations in sci/tech literature and social science literature, respectively.

International Data Corporation - monitors the location of computer facilities in the U.S. and elsewhere identifying central processing units and related facts about each facility. Its market is primarily suppliers of computer room equipment services and supplies.

Predicasts, Inc. - a Cleveland based company, monitors the literature of the business world and captures one-line entries on specific articles industries by SIC code numbers to facilitate users seeking information on specific industrial and business fields.

Disclosure, Inc. of Silver Spring, MD., has created a machine readable file of abstracts covering all the corporate reports required to be filed with the Securities and Exchange Commission. The information files are published regularly in inkprint as a form of bibliographic control over the microfilm version of the documents also marketed by Disclosure. The arrangement was achieved through soliciation of competitive sources by SEC that resulted in a no-cost to the government contract. The latest contract renewal included a provision for pilot programs in Dallas and

---

[5] Both are products of the Institute for Scientific Information, Phila.

Nashville where library use of the financial information provided by Disclosure developed new customers for the libraries. Subsequently, these two libraries have subscribed to the Disclosure Service to continue serving their users.

Standard and Poor's - a McGraw-Hill Company, has collected a great deal of detailed income statement and balance sheet data on public companies, data which were not compiled and easily available anywhere else to the public.

The New York Times Information Bank - includes full texts of the informative abstracts written on all articles appearing in the New York Times.

The government subsidized the creation of a wide-range of sci/tech data bases by professional societies. These include Engineering Index, Chemical Abstracts, American Physics Institute and others.

Many of these information banks are marketed respectively by each company in a variety of formats and initially were offered only in ink-print.

There are a dozen companies which have built information banks, in part based on the MARC tapes, offering a multitude of services to libraries. Information Dynamics Corp., Richard Abel & Co., Science Pres., Inc., Brodait, are but a few.

B.   INFORMATION BANK VENDORS

The last 18 months has seen the emergence of companies marketing access to machine readable information banks. The function of these companies is to make arrangements to have available for on-line search as many information banks as possible. They then seek to develop a dual multi-plier effect in marketing access to these banks. The more banks a company has "up" the easier it is to convince a user to install the necessary terminal equipment by which to gain access to the files. Similarily, the more there is to search the more likely it is the searches will be made.

Lockheed Information Systems, Systems Development Corporation and certain time-sharing organizations such as General Electric vend access to multiple information banks stored in their systems based on a variety of lease and user charges.

Lockheed is experimenting with several Northern California libraries under a National Science Foundation grant to determine the feasibility of having libraries serve as "retail" outlets for these search services. Presumably, the cost of these search services would ultimately have to be borne either by the library or its users.

A further innovation both Lockheed and SDC offer their subscribers who perform searches on information files created by the Institute for Scientific Information is the facility to order a tear sheet of any article they obtain a citation on from the system. The orders are stored in the vendor's computer and are "read out" by ISI at the end of the day. Original Article Tear Sheets or authorized photocopies are supplied by ISI by return mail. This arrangement provides one example of how to deal with the threshhold copyright problem, since ISI has established relationships on copyright questions with, and pay royalties to, the publishers of journals cited in its information bank file.

The New York Times Information Bank is unique in that the creator of the Bank is also vending access to it by placing terminals and training people in their use. The _Times_ is experimenting in Canada with providing individuals access to the files through libraries.

The availability of such services in libraries has numerous side effects:

(1) For information bank creators and vendors who originally designed their service and priced it on a "per-search" basis increased usage in libraries widens the market.

(2) For creators and vendors whose costs have never been subsidized and also serve a narrow market, the ability of users to gain access to the file on a "per-use" basis without paying lease fees charged other users destroys the economic basis of the file and will eventually eliminate its availability or result in severe modification in the file and its marketing procedures.

(3) In some cases where access to the machine readable version requires the use of an ink-print version, library usage will expand markets for both.

(4) In cases where the availability of the machine readable file on a per-use basis is an adequate substitute for the ink-print versions, there is serious cause for concern on the part of the publisher who has an economic activity in ink-print but may lose out if the machine readable file becomes available even on a "per-use" basis in libraries.

C. PUBLISHERS

Libraries are filled with the products of publishers, books, journals, pamphlets, recordings, film strips, microfilm collections. All are economic goods which have been purchased by libraries for the express purpose of lending them to the patrons of the libraries. When these items are out on loan they are off the shelf. If demand increased in the past additional copies were purchased.

In many cases this lending practice created an awareness of the value of the information contained in the materials and often led to individuals subscribing directly on a personal basis for similar services. In the case of many business information services this led to the development of a whole market for timely services.

Many publishers offer discounts to libraries considering the library a ready market and one requiring lesser marketing expense to reach. Other publishers, primarily of reference and information tools scale their subscription rate to the anticipated number of users expected to have access to their products. In any case, the pricing strategy is designed to generate sufficient revenues from a multitude of sources to make it economic to undertake the creation, manufacture and distribution of a particular product.

A starting point for this strategy is the identification of "first copy costs", or what does it cost to create the first copy? (After one copy is made, the incremental costs of subsequent copies are usually comparatively small.) The economics of publishing requires that all subscribers pay a share of these first copy costs. Since the first copy costs are to be incurred, regardless of the medium used for publication, many journal publishers contend that spreading these over the largest ink-print press run possible is the most cost-effective means of distributing scientific and technical information.

In the field of publishing there also is a relatively new phenomonon called micropublishing, or more correctly microrepublishing, since it almost universally involves republishing ink-print materials, both under copyright and in the public domain, in microform.

Information Handling Services organizes, indexes, and microfilms on

15 mm cartridge film engineering and construction catalog information. Its contribution is to organize and make readily accessible a large body of otherwise elusive and quickly dated materials.

Congressional Information Service abstracts, indexes and microfilms nearly one-half the total output of the Government Printing Office. Two basic corpura of documents includes all Congressionally generated reports, hearings, bills, etc. (except The Congressional Record which is microrepublished by University Microfilms, Princeton Microfilms and others) and statistical publications of all government agencies. CIS recently began offering a file containing copies of all bills offered in Congress at a price substantially below the product of the Library of Congress it replaced. Its breakeven point is approximately 15 subscribers. (In the information service environment small audiences can be served economically and competitively.)

Readex Microprint republishers the complete output of the Government Printing Office in a micro-opaque medium for which it also offers a reader/printer.

Research Publications, Inc. collects and microfilms large academic collections such as the Papers of The Confederacy and the League of Nations Documents. It also offers a microfilm on all patents issued by The Patent Office and has began filming state documents. It provides detailed indexes with which to use its products.

University Microfilms, has collected U. S. doctoral theses on microfilm and has created a Dissertations Abstracts publication by which to identify relevant theses. It also markets to libraries authorized microfilm versions of most popular periodicals.

Bell and Howell Microphoto microfilms large numbers of newspapers including a whole collection on the underground press.

Greenwood Press micropublishers large collections of a retrospective nature and also offers a service on municipal documents.

Disclosure, Inc., U.S. Historical Documents Institute, Microfilming Corporation of America and Library Resources, also offer a variety of micro-published materials.

This is a relatively new industry dating back only to the years immediately prior to World War 2. It is an industry that has learned that to stay in business it must do more than create on film that which already exists in ink-print; it must add value by what it does. This value most often takes the form of one or all of the following:

(1) Collecting as complete a set as humanly possible from many disparate sources.

(2) Organizing, editing and arranging the material.

(3) Filming and coding the material on film.

(4) Creating tools by which users can locate on the microfilm the precise information they desire promptly and easily.

In many cases the first copy costs of these collections must be spread over a maximum expected sale of 15 to 20 copies.

D. INFORMATION BY-PRODUCTS

These include everything from SDI services to journals, newsletters and other serial products. They might be by-products of an information bank or a micropublishing or publishing venture.

One major business---Dodge Information Systems--a McGraw-Hill Company, fits in this category. The Dodge people serve the construction field. They have a data base consisting of all construction jobs being undertaken in the U.S. of a certain minimum size. The file contains information such as date bids are due, who was awarded the contract, when various subcontracts will be let, who the subcontractor is and when he is expected to buy light bulbs, etc.

Information is sold out of this file to all kinds of users who wish to compete for the business of supplying materials to builders. This is sold in little pieces of paper on a daily basis, on user pre-printed multiple copy computer forms for use by salesmen and their managers in keeping track of business in a territory, etc.

Obviously, this information gives a salesman great control over who he is and what he can become. It has great value.

Newsletters are another "by-product," but more a by-product of the data base building process than of the completed data base. A newsletter has value because it becomes built into the user's life style. It repeatedly gives him ideas and concepts that are relevant. The newsletter publisher maintains good "feed back" from his users and knows whether what he puts out is used, and, if not, why not, and how to correct it. That is data base building. People who have been doing this for a long time have a natural reserve of information that should be convertible to a data base.

This, in turn, can then be repackaged as books, as SDI, as on-line retrieval information, as complementary data bases to other files also "up" on the same system, etc. While there are data conversion costs involved, the most expensive functions--data acquisition and editing--have been done and paid for. In addition the information has been validated through demonstration and repeated use.

Information is a non-depleting resource and, in fact, its use enhances its value for users as well as for information publishing companies.

E. INFORMATION EVALUATION

It, too, embraces a multitude of activities. It includes, for example, facilities management, such as the Informatics operation of the NASA Space Information Center, where the world of space-related information is evaluated, managed and distributed. Herner & Co. runs a similar facility for Walter Reed Army Medical Center, concentrating on managing bio-medical research results for the U.S. Army. Aspen Systems has operated more limited facilities for specific task-oriented activities creating an information capability in support of certain inquiries by regulatory agencies of government.

Another example of the information evaluation activities of the industry is the whole phenomenon of "user generated", or custom query "on demand" information companies. A prime example is FIND, operated by Information Clearing House, N. Y. There are probably 20-30 companies of this kind in the U.S. today operating on a commercial basis. There are at least as many operated by government and non-profit ventures as well.

The economic reality giving rise to this business is the multi-disciplinary approach all businesses are forced to take today. Libraries in business locations turn out to have finite personnel and holdings. Rather than augment both and build into their cost structure permanent high levels of activities, many businesses are choosing to rely on the "expert access"

Originally page 17 ERIC

to information these firms provide. (They serve a similar function to that of the temporary help firms.)

In addition, if one of these on-demand companies has 500 industrial subscribers it probably recognizes that to be a valid statistical sample of the U.S. market for information. If a dozen companies out of those 500 ask about the same question in one week, this triggers certain developments: (1) The question is researched 12 different ways. (2) The researchers identify the fact that this subject probably is of interest to a large number of other companies, both subscribers and non-subscribers. (3) A special report is prepared as a by-product of the earlier research and is sold. (4) The research itself, without regard to the source of the questions, may be used to construct a data base for other users as well.

Also in this information evaluation field is the whole area of special reports such as those created by Frost & Sullivan, Predicasts, Quantum Science, International Data Corporation, Auerbach, Business International, etc. In the sense that specialized (mostly sci/tech) journals also carry evaluated (by peers) information, they too fall in this category.

III – TRADITIONAL LIBRARY/INDUSTRY RELATIONSHIPS

In the age of evolving reading literacy library/industry relations were mutually beneficial.

Libraries were and still are for many companies the principal market for published products. For many products, the existance of a fairly certain library market for a book or journal assured a large press run distributing first copy costs widely and reducing retail prices for individuals as a result.

.   Libraries with collections of materials and subscriptions to current
periodicals also form a market for publishers of reference works and for
current awareness services. Both such products rely on the ready availability within the library of a fulfillment capability to complete the
current awareness/fulfillment cycle essential to the complete information
process.

For newer, innovative products libraries offer the traditional service of training individual users in the use of new products.

IV — TRANSITIONAL LIBRARY/INDUSTRY RELATIONSHIPS

What is characterized in the Report as the threshhold question –
copyright – covers a wide range of ways in which the library/industry roles
are in transition.

For the journal publisher, interlibrary loans via photocopies represents a reversal of the relationship by which sufficiently large press
runs resulted in distributing first copy costs broadly over all or almost
all users. Current practice resulting in reduced multiple subscriptions
within each library have drastically reduced the number of subscriptions
from which first copy costs can be recovered.

The further practice of photocopying portions of journals, thereby
eliminating the need for users or satellite or borrowing libraries to subscribe has the following result. (See Figure 4).

Publishing & Use Cycle

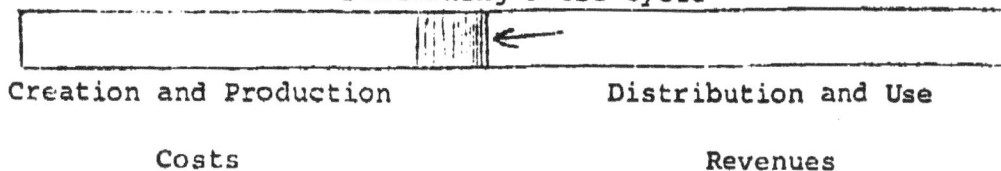

Creation and Production	Distribution and Use
Costs	Revenues

In the publishing and use cycle the major costs are associated with creation and production. Revenues are generated from the distribution and use end. Photocopying, while not generating revenues for libraries, does push the publisher farther and farther back into the cost area and out of distribution and revenue area.

In many situations libraries by marketing their services to commercial users in industrialized locations on a subsidized basis are competing unfairly with firms which must recover capital investment, pay a return on investment (prime rates remain high for venture capital), and pay state and federal taxes. The change represented by this example is one of scale of activity rather than in kind. Often in order to "get a good return for the taxpayers investment in a new information service" libraries will seek to reach out to precisely the same people to whom the private sector is seeking to market similar or even identical services.

Superficially, both are serving the same objective - raising the information literacy of the U.S. population. From an economic standpoint, however, there is a real danger that this kind of unfair competition will destroy the economic viability of the creator of the service involved and his business will fail. Government funding will become the only viable way of creating such information services. By comparison, consider what the

Originally page 20 ERIC

Originally page 🖙 Zurkowski

impact on freedom of expression would have been as the U.S. developed reading literacy if government funding had been the only viable way of publishing books and journals.

A major feature of transitional library/industry relations, thus, is that both libraries and information companies are seeking to serve the same users of very specialized services.

This would be further aggravated by the creation of a national system for sharing resources unless ways were clearly defined for achieving optimum utilization of both resources.

Other than photocopying is involved in this area. For a micropublisher of a large academic collection of materials, the sharing among major research libraries of key portions of the microfilmed collections can be fatal to the economic viability of the collection if as much as one of the 15-20 potential sales are lost. A national system of sharing would guarantee that result in every case. Here again specific ways must be found to assure continued viability of multiple sources of materials.

In the case of federal libraries their redesignation as information centers also represents a real threat not only to industry but to the national tax base as well. Many federal information centers offer subsidized information services to an ever widening circle of users - first, other government agencies, then, state agencies, then, government contractors, then, their subcontractors and then on ad infinitum.

Not only does this preempt large markets for direct sales to these same users of information services, but it creates a larger federal bureaucy and denies tax revenues to both state and federal treasuries.

It is significant that the first Congressional policy statement on government competition with the private sector should have come in 1933. In the depth of a depression, when Congress was cutting its salaries, it is logical that the Congress would recognize the hazards to the tax base of government agency preemption of private sector opportunities.

The size of the impact on tax revenues was set forth in a Department of Commerce table at 60 of the Report of the Commission on Government Procurement. The Commerce Department estimated that in 1970 there were $4 billion of services performed by the government that could have been shifted to the private sector.

The report states this would have produced an additional $25 to $35 million in tax revenues to the states alone. In fiscal 1970 the government agencies reported $7 billion of similar services that were performed in house rather than contracted out. If $5 billion of that had been shifted to the private sector the taxes paid to the U.S. Treasury would have totalled up to $250 million.

V – POLICY QUESTIONS

In the "Reading Service Environment" the basic policy issue: what portion of publishing and library services should be left to be satisfied by operation of the forces of the marketplace and what portion must be subsidized was fairly clearly defined. In fact, the subsidized portion operating by resource sharing aggregated dependable, continuously-funded markets for publishers who, thus, became secondary beneficiaries of the subsidy. Economics of size were assured and a stable, well-balanced system evolved to serve the reading public.

This complex of relationships constituting the Reading Service Environ-

Originally page **22** Zurkowski

Originally page ?? Zurkowski

ment in the main provided a healthy, dynamic institutional framework for harnessing the nation's pluralistic resources to the task of creating a reading literate society and a competitive marketplace of ideas. In many respects this relationship still pertains and it is in the public interest for all concerned to continue to build on this mutuality of interest in extending information literacy to the all segments of society.

With the introduction of new information processing technologies the line between marketplace and subsidized functions in some respects has become blurred. The process of achieving information literacy involves defining that line clearly and realistically, and in defining an institutional framework for the Information Service Environment. In our age of information overabundance, being information literate means being able to find what is known or knowable on any subject. The tools and techniques and the organizations providing them for doing that form this institutional framework. Three major time tested policies contributed to the success of the Reading Service Environment and their application to the Information Service Environment is essential to its successful operation:

1. Individual fulfillment, the advancement of knowledge and the discovering of truth, participation in decision making by all members of society, and achieving an adaptable and stable community depends on a system of freedom of expression. [6]

2. Government should not perform services for citizens which citizens are capable of performing for themselves.

3. Government has a legitimate responsibility for assuring educational opportunities for all.

[6] Thomas I. Emerson, _The System of Freedom of Expression_, Random House, 1970, p. 3 et seq.

A. THE SYSTEM OF FREEDOM OF EXPRESSION
BASIS FOR THE INFORMATION SERVICE ENVIRONMENT

"Congress shall make no law...abridging the freedom of speech or of the press...." First Amendment, U. S. Constitution.

"A system of freedom of expression * * * is a group of rights assured to individual members of the society to form and hold beliefs and opinions on any subject, and to communicate ideas, opinions and information through any medium * * * from the obverse side it includes the right to hear the views of others and to listen to their version of the facts. * * * the full benefits of the system can be realized only when the individual knows the extent of his rights and has some assurance of protection in exercising them. * * * it does not come naturally to the ordinary citizen, but needs to be learned. It must be restated and reiterated not only for each generation but for each new situation. It leans heavily upon understanding and education, both for the individual and the community as a whole.

"Thus it is clear that the problem of maintaining a system of freedom of expression is one of the most complex any society has to face, self-restraint, self-discipline, and maturity are required. * * * The members of society must be willing to sacrifice individual and short-term advantage for social and long-range goals.

"Second (among legal doctrines supporting a system of freedom of expression) is the utilization and simultaneous restriction of government in regulating conflicts between individuals or groups within the system of free expression; in protecting individuals or groups from non-government interference in the exercise of their right to expression; and in eliminating obstacles to, or affirmatively promoting effective functioning of the system. * * * Development of this concept involves formulating specific rules for mutual accommodation of participants in the system, fairness in allocation of scarce facilities and assurance that the system will be expanded rather than contracted." [7]

The practical policy implications for achieving information literacy of a system of freedom of expression are:

(1) Resource sharing in the Information Service Environment differs by an order of magnitude and has the opposite impact on sources

[7] Thomas I. Emerson, The System of Freedom of Expressing op cit.

Originally page 24 ERIC

BEST COPY AVAILABLE

of materials to that which it had in the Reading Service Environment. In-stead of aggregating markets for suppliers of materials it disaggregates these markets and denies compensation to suppliers for their services. This destroys the economic foundations of the suppliers and reduces plur-alism in choices available to citizens. Systematic photocopying of pub-lished materials amounts to republishing and requires copyright clearances. All parties should work together to resolve this threshhold question.

(2) In-house or captive development of systems capability denies the entire (not just the library) community the benefit of competition among suppliers. (Services developed outside the library community can be sold to non-library users and the cost be amortized more broadly.) Services for inter-library cooperation should not be contracted for on a sole source basis. Competitive procurement should be required to ob-tain competitive bids on the specifically described services desired.

(3) A concommitant of freedom of expression is the need for the user to have confidence in the information source on which he proposes to rely. Subsidization of activities that preempt alternative sources eliminates one base for confidence: Competition among products delivering concepts and ideas.

(4) Individuals require not only the right to speak, but also to be heard. A pluralism of channels for communication must therefore be pre-served. This will require restraint on the part of subsidized activities so as not to preempt opportunity or to eliminate channels for communication alternative to subsidized channels.

(5) There must be a clear policy statement favoring alternative

channels for communication since in its absence the risk capital needed to sustain alternate channels will not be forthcoming. For pluralism to be assured, there must be assurance that the system will be expanded rather than contracted.

B. GOVERNMENT SERVICES

Government should not perform services for its citizens which the citizens are capable of performing themselves. The benefits of this policy are:

(1) That private, competitive services arise to offer citizens a choice of services.

(2) That the private services offered amortize first copy costs against all possible users rather than only those government would serve with its products.

(3) That the tax base is broadened by policies encouraging private initiatives and the investment of private risk capital in the development of capital intensive activities.

(4) That it is more cost-effective for government to rely on private risk capital investments. If one agency requires a service needing $2 million in capital investment, by relying on private risk capital it can reduce its costs to a pro rata share of that cost distributed among all users.

The Government of the U.S. also has the responsibility to assure that the opportunity for private sector initiatives is expanded and not contracted. This should be implemented through policies affecting the procurement policies and competitive activities of the instrumentalities the government chooses to fund to implement its objectives.

Since there currently is no national agency charged with the responsibility for overseeing the formulation, implementation and oversight of government policies in this area, it is all the more important that the

Originally page 26 ERIC

Originally page 26 Zurkowski

Commission enunciate a policy identifying goals for government activities in the information service field which will direct the energies of people in government in supportive rather than competitive activities.

C. EDUCATION

Much of what has been stated above pertains to the estimated one-sixth of the U. S. Population that is information literate. The priorities of the Commission should be directed toward facilitating the participation of the pluralistic segments of the Information Service Environment already serving that segment of society. Capital investment by government in developing further resources to serve that share of the population would necessarily come at the expense of the five-sixths of the population that lacks the training to be literate in an information sense.

The top priority of the Commission should be directed toward establishing a major national program to achieve universal information literacy by 1984.

This would involve the coordination and funding of a massive effort to train all citizens in the use of the information tools now available as well as those in the development and testing states. The pattern of growth in this field is well established and should be built upon to expand the overall capability of all U.S. Citizens. Such an effort would necessarily create many new opportunities, some of which would be appropriate to the marketplace and others for subsidy.

Until the population as a whole is prepared to utilize and benefit across the board from the capabilities of the Information Service Environment proposals to create systems serving the elite alone will lack the popular political support needed to obtain the level of government funding suggested in the Report of the Commission.

Glossary

Action literacy- the ability to transform good content into ethical action. Being action literate means that one's ethical actions are consistently rooted in good information. The actions are helpful. The actions are good. Right actions are carried out even when difficult

Critical thinking- using questions to evaluate and create good value from information. Questioning accuracy, authenticity, context, clarity and relevance are examples of actions that help achieve good value from information

Disinformation- knowingly providing false or distracting/deceptive information

Information asymmetry [coined by George Akerlof, 1970]- in contract theory and economics, information asymmetry deals with the study of decisions in transactions where one party has more or better information than the other. This creates an imbalance of power in transactions [definition by John O. Ledyard]

Information equivalence- information that accurately represents something in a form different from that something. A photograph, a schematic and architectural plans are examples. DNA and genes are other examples

Information literacy- 1. The ability to extract, accept, and create good value from needed information [Jeffrey Kelly]. 2. Techniques and skills for utilizing the wide range of information tools as well as primary sources in molding information solutions to ones problems. Taking information from knowledge to understanding to wisdom [Zurkowski]. Being information literate or not is dependent upon context: Most indigenous Arctic people, information literate in the ways of the Arctic, would be information *illiterate* if dropped into Harvard Yard just as most students from Harvard Yard would be information *illiterate* if dropped next to an ice hole or a herd of reindeer in the Arctic

Information overload- whenever available information exceeds ones capacity to evaluate it [Zurkowski, *Related Paper No. 5*, ERIC p. 1, 1974]

Misinformation- providing false information that is harmful without first checking its veracity